Business Strategy in the Artificial Intelligence Economy

Business Strategy in the Artificial Intelligence Economy

Edited by

J. Mark Munoz and Al Naqvi

BUSINESS EXPERT PRESS

Business Strategy in the Artificial Intelligence Economy

First published in 2018 by
Business Expert Press, LLC
222 East 46th Street, New York, NY 10017
www.businessexpertpress.com

ISBN-13: 978-1-94819-898-1 (paperback)
ISBN-13: 978-1-94819-899-8 (e-book)

Business Expert Press Strategic Management Collection

Collection ISSN: 2150-9611 (print)
Collection ISSN: 2150-9646 (electronic)

Cover and interior design by Exeter Premedia Services Private Ltd., Chennai, India

First edition: 2018

10 9 8 7 6 5 4 3 2 1

Printed in the United States of America.

Abstract

Technological breakthroughs relating to artificial intelligence has redefined business operations worldwide. For example, the ways in which data are captured, processed, and utilized to optimize customer interactions have grown by leaps and bounds. The change is redefining the structural dynamics of business strategy, economic theory, and management concepts. Leading technology companies around the world have expanded their research in artificial intelligence. With IBM's launch of Watson, a new Cognitive Era has started. Investment firms have backed numerous emerging artificial intelligence companies. Meanwhile, there is paucity of academic and business research on the subject. This book project is a pioneering examination of how artificial intelligence is transforming the contemporary business strategy.

Keywords

artificial intelligence, business strategy, strategy

Contents

CHAPTER 1

Introduction

Al Naqvi and J. Mark Munoz

The race to gain a decisive and astounding jump of 40 percent in productivity (Purdy and Daugherty 2016) is on. The world is seeking a solution to its productivity woes and the answer lies in the rise of Artificial Intelligence (AI). The growth of AI is rapid, selective, and impromptu. Each of the three factors is a super volcano waiting to erupt and its eruption will create major and uncontrollable tectonic change in the social, economic, and political order. Unmanaged entry into the fourth, and perhaps the final, industrial revolution may have consequences for both who dare to embrace and those who stay on the sidelines. But regardless of the choice made, no one will be able to escape the ominous rise of the AI. The proliferation of AI has taken place in stages. The changes that took place as well as their implications are described in the following sections.

The Rapid Rise

AI has been around for at least 60 years and has gone through waves of optimism followed by disappointing results and investment stagnation. Much to the annoyance of investors, it often overpromised and underdelivered. Back in the research labs AI community continued to work diligently to expand the field. Fortunes changed when data revolution enhanced the processing capacity and provided access to tremendous data. It was as if an oxygen-deprived person breathing through a hose suddenly woke up and began running a marathon in a planet full of oxygen. The winter of AI lifted, never to return. Developments in mathematical algorithms contributed to the creation of machine learning by leaps and bounds and the AI revolution was born. This time around though, it was not going back. All that it needed was here, and all that remained was to create more and more intelligence. The concentration and integration of various interdependent technologies led to the emergence of the new revolution. Billions are being invested and the pace of innovation and related applications is increasing at an exponential rate. The world is not ready to embrace the technology and perhaps the technology is not ready to embrace the world but that is not stopping the ongoing amalgamation of the two. The fast and furious introduction of the technology is outpacing the ability to develop and deploy legal and regulatory frameworks and governance mechanisms.

The Selective Rise

AI is developing selectively across countries, cities, and regions. This inequitable induction of technology will give tremendous intellectual and financial advantage to certain areas while reducing the competitive advantage of others. Cognitively advanced systems when combined with advanced robotics will be able to perform complex work. The cities and countries that will be home to these technologies (and the firms developing them) will create an unconquerable competitive disparity between themselves and the rest of the world. Such a gap will not close since the advantage of technology leaders will grow exponentially.

The Impromptu Rise

The developments are fast and unplanned. More than anything else, AI is poised to increase global unemployment. Productivity increase implies job loss for many. Raising the alarms of unemployment is often conveniently rejected by labeling the harbingers as nihilists or Luddites. This is a mistake. The authors have argued in other papers that the lessons from the previous industrial revolutions cannot be applied in the current revolution. The differences are significant. First, unlike other technologies, the AI technology can learn and optimize. Second, the AI technology may soon be able to adapt and respond to its environment in a significantly powerful way than the traditional machines. Once self-driving autonomous cabs are out on the roads, the entire cab-driving profession will be wiped out. And it is unlikely that all or most of those out-of-work cab drivers will be retrained as AI engineers. Plain and simple, what is needed is a planned rollout such that social and economic costs are minimized.

Contemporary Artificial Intelligence (AI) Environment

The Obama administration attempted to create an agenda for the artificial intelligence technology. It is expected that the Trump administration will also continue to support the development of the field. The Obama administration analyzed the rise of the big data technology and then followed it by separate analysis of the AI revolution. Two reports were issued by the White House and both recorded the perils and promises of AI (White House 2016al; 2016b). In the end, however, the optimism of promises prevailed over the perils of the technology as the U.S. government set a road map for progress in AI. With its eyes on the potential productivity gains of an incredible 40 percent (Purdy and Daugherty 2016), the U.S. government wasted no time to give unconditional support to the industry. Relentless pursuit of technological progress ensued as billions of dollars of private investment poured into the AI field.

When the monster comes out of the bush, there will be some damage. Frey and Osborne calculated that just about half the jobs can be impacted (Frey and Osborne 2013). Brynjolfsson and McAfee (2015) have observed that the four measures of economic health, per capita gross domestic product (GDP), labor productivity, number of jobs, and median household income, tend to grow in tandem but not in the last 15 or so years. GDP and productivity have parted ways with income and jobs, as the first two have increased but the latter two have declined. They call it decoupling (Brynjolfsson and McAfee 2015; McAfee and Brynjolfsson 2016). Others have acknowledged that the need for high-skill jobs would grow but what is rated as a high-skill job today may not sustain such a classification for far too long (Autor 2015; Autor and Dorn 2013).

AI enables productivity enhancement, changes work processes, and can create jobs (Rao 2017). New technologies threaten about 40 percent of jobs in the United States and approximately two-thirds of those in the developing world (Gershon 2017). A report from Ball State University showed that in the United States almost 9 out of 10 jobs were lost to robots and not to trade (Hicks and Devaraj 2015). If this is some indication of how things will look in the future, job creation might become extremely hard. So, the ill-fated dilemma takes shape. If jobs go to humans, that means the United States will be less productive than global competitors and may miss out on the 40 percent productivity potential. If jobs go to robots, then how will the country create new middle-class jobs?

There is a high interest in AI and the future is promising. Due to its impact on product variety, personalization, attractiveness, and cost benefits, AI will contribute to 45 percent of all economic gains by 2030 (PWC 2016). Nesbitt (2017) indicated that AI impacts trade by: (1) enabling supply chains, (2) creating efficiency in compliance software, (3) speeding up and creating better contracts, and (4) improving access to finance.

Support for AI has been evident. There were about 1,500 AI-related start-ups in the United States in 2016, receiving funding of around $5 billion (Rao 2017).

Other types of support are necessary for AI to thrive. There needs to be a strong AI program, which should have full support of the government. However, it is strongly recommended that such a program be monitored and governed so that advance policy steps can be taken before masses are exposed to the consequential suffering. Of course, this implies the development of an exceptionally powerful safety net program as well as other programs to support retraining and continuing education. An extremely strong focus on education specific to AI is critical and highly recommended.

Book Objectives and Structure

The objective of this book is to capture the viewpoints of thought leaders from around the world and share their ideas on business strategy formation in a world of AI. Given that there is scarce literature on the subject, this pioneering book aims to break through conventional management wisdom and recalibrate business thinking in order to best adapt to an evolving technological terrain.

This book offers high value to a multitude of audiences. Academics would find the topics relevant to discussions and debates on contemporary business strategy and management. Corporate executives will find the topics helpful in the implementation of viable management approaches in a technology-driven world. Entrepreneurs can derive innovative ideas for ventures in AI. Business consultants will be able to enhance value for their clients by identifying additional areas for operational enhancement. Government officials, executives of international organizations, and policy makers worldwide will find new ideas in this book that can help improve business and economic growth.

The book is organized in such a way that the reader is exposed to a diverse set of business functions that impact strategy in a world of AI. The broad range of topics offers the reader an array of tools to use to assess, analyze, and identify solutions for technological and organizational challenges.

The book has 11 chapters : Chapter 1: Introduction (*Al Naqvi and J. Mark Munoz*), Chapter 2: The role of AI in the knowledge organization of companies (*Andrea Bencsik*), Chapter 3: A new perspective of change for the AI age (*Krishna Raj Bhandari*), Chapter 4: AI in strategic human resources management (*Al Naqvi*), Chapter 5: AI and cybersecurity (*Mehrdad Sharbaf*), Chapter 6: AI and innovation management (*Carlos Agustin Vazquez Hernandez*), Chapter 7: Permissionless evolution of ethics—AI (*Margaret Goralski and Krystyna Gorniak-Kocikowska*), Chapter 8: The future of logistics and marketing in an AI-governed world (*Luis Soto and Sergio Biggemann*), Chapter 9: AI and customer service in health care (*Norrie Daroga*), Chapter 10: AI-based decision making applied in marketing and sales in third world countries (*Abel Kinoti Meru, Felix Musau, and Mary Wanjiru Kinoti*), and Chapter 11: Conclusion (*J. Mark Munoz and Al Naqvi*).

Artificial intelligence is the new, and perhaps the final, frontier for the decisive casting of competitiveness. Any country or company that wants to remain, or become, competitive must launch a powerful and planned AI development, rollout, adoption, and diffusion program. This book, through the following chapters, offers innovative ideas in business strategy, which provides the foundation for capturing new competitive advantages.

There are some important points that are captured in the book:

1. Artificial intelligence is not just a change; it is a revolution (analogous to the industrial revolution).
2. When thinking about strategy, the rise of AI needs to be approached from the three levels of strategy: corporate-level strategy, business unit-level strategy, and functional-level (departmental-level) strategy.
3. Artificial intelligence is an irreversible change and the technology has matured to have a highly impactful and meaningful contribution in the world.
4. Business strategy development process should take into account AI as the main focus of strategy development.
5. Launching an AI or cognitive transformation program is not easy. It needs to be done carefully and meticulously.
6. Ethics are an important part of the transformation and models of ethics and governance are needed to lead the transformation.
7. Technological architectures designed for the information age era may need to be upgraded for the cognitive era.
8. A clear and comprehensive strategy is needed from the government (governments) to ensure that the cognitive revolution succeeds and that the negative socioeconomic impact is minimized.

AI will set the stage for economic transformation and disruption and will be the foundation for new competitive advantages (PWC 2016). For instance, pediatrician Dr. Harvey Karp, Yves Behar, and MIT-trained engineers created a bassinet (almost a robotic crib) called Snoo that comforts newborns through white noise, movement, and sensation of being swaddled (Kelly 2017). The Climate Corporation has an advanced autonomous AI app that converges information on climate, farm yield, and insurance to create a cost-effective and operationally efficient automated claims process (Rao 2017). Amazon's Echo uses Alexa, a chatbot, to interact with customers (Baraniuk 2017). These are just a few examples of how AI is transforming businesses and lives worldwide.

AI and the advancement that it brings impact the world of business in many ways. There is much to learn with regard to the extent, breadth, and depth of its impact. This book starts this investigative journey and aims to set the foundation to best manage and strategize in a world of AI.

References

Autor, D.H. 2015. "Why are there Still So Many Jobs? The History and Future of Workplace Automation." *The Journal of Economic Perspectives* 29, no. 3, 3–30. [online], available from http://ingentaconnect.com/content/aea/jep/2015/00000029/00000003/art00001

Autor, D.H., and D. Dorn. 2013. "The Growth of Low Skill Service Jobs and the Polarization of the U.S. Labor Market." *American Economic Review* 103, no. 5, 1553–97. [Online].

Baraniuk, C. 2017. "Could Robots Put an End to Maddening Customer Service Calls?" available at http://bbc.com/capital/story/20170706-could-robots-put-an-end-to-maddening-customer-service-calls (accessed September 20, 2017).

Brynjolfsson, E., and A. McAfee. 2015. "Will Humans Go the Way of Horses? Labor in the Second Machine Age." *Foreign Affairs* 94, no. 4.

Frey, C.B., and M.A. Osborne. 2013. "The Future of Employment: How Susceptible are Jobs to Computerisation?" *Technological Forecasting and Social Change* 114, pp. 254–80.

Gershon, L. 2017. "The Automation Resistant Skills We Should Nurture." *BBC*, available at http://bbc.com/capital/story/20170726-the-automation-resistant-skills-we-should-nurture (accessed September 20, 2017).

Hicks, M.J., and S. Devaraj. 2015. *The Myth and Reality of Manufacturing in America*. [online], available from: http://conexus.cberdata.org/files/MfgReality.pdf%0D. [online], available from http://conexus.cberdata.org/files/MfgReality.pdf%0D

Kelly, S.M. 2017. "A Robotic Crib Rocked My Baby to Sleep for Months." *CNN Tech*, available at http://money.cnn.com/2017/08/10/technology/gadgets/snoo-review/index.html?iid=ob_homepage_tech_pool (accessed September 20, 2017).

McAfee, A., and E. Brynjolfsson. 2016. "Human Work in the Robotic Future." *Foreign Affairs* 95, no. 4, pp. 139–50. [online], available from http://search.ebscohost.com/login.aspx?direct=true&db=ssa&AN=115986098&site=ehost-live

Nesbitt, J. 2017. "4 Ways Artificial Intelligence Is Transforming Trade." available at http://tradeready.ca/2017/topics/import-export-trade-management/4-ways-artificial-intelligence-transforming-trade/ (accessed September 21, 2017).

Purdy, M., and P. Daugherty. October 2016. "Why Artificial Intelligence is the Future of Growth?" *Remarks at AI Now: The Social and Economic Implications of Artificial Intelligence Technologies in the Near Term*, 1–72. [online], available from https://accenture.com/_acnmedia/PDF-19/AI_in_Management_Report.pdf#zoom=50

PWC 2016. "Sizing the Prize: PWC's Global Artificial Intelligence Study: Exploiting the AI Revolution." available at https://pwc.com/gx/en/issues/data-and-analytics/publications/artificial-intelligence-study.html (accessed September 21, 2017).

Rao, A. 2017. "A Strategist's Guide to Artificial Intelligence." *Strategy + Business*, available at https://strategy-business.com/article/A-Strategists-Guide-to-Artificial-Intelligence?gko=0abb5&utm_source=itw&utm_medium=20170523&utm_campaign=respB (accessed September 20, 2017).

White House 2016a. *Artificial Intelligence, Automation, and the Economy*. [online], available from https://obamawhitehouse.archives.gov/sites/whitehouse.gov/files/documents/Artificial-Intelligence-Automation-Economy.PDF. [online], available from https://obamawhitehouse.archives.gov/sites/whitehouse.gov/files/documents/Artificial-Intelligence-Automation-Economy.PDF

White House 2016b. *Preparing for the Future of Artificial Intelligence*. [online], available from https://obamawhitehouse.archives.gov/sites/default/files/whitehouse_files/microsites/ostp/NSTC/preparing_for_the_future_of_ai.pdf

CHAPTER 2

The Role of Artificial Intelligence in the Knowledge Organization of Companies

Andrea Bencsik

Introduction

The increased importance of human resources, knowledge, and intellectual capital figure is a challenge for organizations in a competitive business environment. The primary challenge is the maximum utilization of the intellectual capital by requiring professional organization of knowledge. The question is how to capture and utilize the knowledge and experience stored in human brain? How can accumulated knowledge be used? This challenge indicated the development of IT systems that are intended to provide access to documentable knowledge and information. Real business success requires development of integrated systems that can answer all the issues of knowledge management (availability, sharing, development, storage, utilization, and completing strategic objectives). This integrated system is not just a standard enterprisewide development and use of IT solutions, but a new way of utilizing human resources and intellectual capital. It has moved the organization toward the creation of a new knowledge-based organization and building knowledge management system (KMS).

Theoretical Background

"There is nothing new under the sun" might be an applicable statement since knowledge management is not a recent phenomenon. The KMS is a new system approach and way of thinking that refines the previous views and management tools.

The development and historical stages of KMS are mainly based on the study of Anklam (2005). In his opinion, the evolutionary stages of knowledge management have been completed and currently the development is in phase six.

The first phase is characterized by a focus on technology anchored on generating knowledge (Nonaka and Takeuchi 1995) with the end in view of knowledge utilization. Knowledge is viewed as a product and information is referred to as a resource.

The main characteristic of the second phase is a conscious handling and recognition of differences in knowledge-based, experiential and problem-solving knowledge. The problematic question is how to encourage the human resources to share their knowledge (Poór 2010).

In the third phase, knowledge is perceived as a network (Chena et al. 2014), where the cooperating organizational partners integrate business models, complex structures, and innovation system groups.

The fourth phase following the classification of Anklam focuses on knowledge as a capital factor and is trying to quantify it, while the fifth phase focuses on the relation between corporate competitiveness and innovation. It is clear that developed economies in the fourth and the fifth phase are looking for the importance of the value of human resources. The current highest level of development is phase six (not yet defined by experts, but seemingly feasible), which due to the effects of Industry 4.0 and digitalization highlights the inevitability of artificial intelligence (AI) (Barkovics 2016). Each step of the KMS system involves those new solutions, which find a solution for problems with the help of digital technology that could not be handled by early IT systems.

The question is how will development proceed. One possible option is the return to the first phase (dominance of IT system building) where IT will gain importance in a new form. With cloud-based solutions, AI will take over the dominance, providing solutions to the questions and problems formulated earlier. There is talk about cyclically repeating demands, but always at a higher level. The earlier phases of development are emerging again, but in the form of KMS supported by AI. The value of human knowledge in this context comes to different light and the possibilities of system building with the support of AI also require a new way of thinking. The other option is to continue the progress and reach phase seven of development, where the effects and expectations can be hardly predictable.

The mentioned phase evolved sequentially as a natural consequence of development of technology and thinking. Nowadays, one can see a positive experience and initiatives in companies representing countries with different culture and level of development, which responding to the expectations of Industry 4.0 can act as best practice for others (Bencsik 2013).

In the following sections, the logic where building KMS is treated as a self-returning cyclical development process will be shown. With the help of this approach, an illustration of how KMS steps can be combined with the possibilities provided by digitalization, that is, how to integrate the solutions of AI into the process of corporate knowledge management, will be shown. An example on how the logic supported by AI can be implemented will be provided. Finally, a summary of possible solutions and methods that paired with the tools applying KMS from a table will be provided.

Knowledge Management System Model

The definition of KM defines an activity chain that presents the knowledge management as a progressing, evolving, and cyclical process (Davenport 1996; Duhon 1998; Gholami et al. 2013). This logic focuses on developing and managing the organizational knowledge base. One of the best-known models was developed by Probst et al. (2006). It consists of eight components that can be divided into external and internal cycles. The individual components are interconnected and form a system based on a logical principle. Following the logic of the model the content requirements of the elements are introduced.

External Cycle

Knowledge Objectives

The knowledge management objectives determine what kind and level of skills and knowledge to develop and use to reach organizational objectives for the next strategic period. Different objectives should be selected at different levels: normative, strategic, and operative.

AI helps with setting objectives, especially in case of "what if" type of questions. Systems supporting strategic decisions bring rules and logic to process data sets. It helps the automation of certain decision-making situations and is also suitable to prepare forecasts (one possible tool is "SAP Digital Boardroom" digital decision support on three screens).

The next phases of the KMS model are always connected to the phase before. This is a start of the internal cycle, including the following six steps.

Internal Cycle

Identification of Knowledge

This component of the model involves an overview of the existing organizational skills and knowledge capital. Before starting a new project, it is necessary to map the existing knowledge. Nowadays, information technology makes it possible to store data exactly in a form it was created. To make the knowledge more transparent, it can be helpful to use tools that can provide an overview about the availability of necessary knowledge (Hanako 2016).

As corporate knowledge is expanding rapidly, a teachable AI system can be established. This system would enable access to customized corporate knowledge. After submitting the required information and based on the answers provided for questions, the system will automatically be able to build the organizational knowledge base, which will automatically be extended with new information (Az öntanító AI 2017). A single, self-learning system will prevent the loss of information, will remember and put each of the knowledge items into the appropriate place. It will keep the organizational knowledge up to date and the holders of knowledge can achieve strategic objectives or the system can be customized to search for information from external sources (SAP HANA solution).

Knowledge Acquisition

Useful information is acquired through formal and informal channels in the company and will make finding knowledged individuals essential for the organization. These channels can be used internally and externally (Davenport and Prusak 2001).

Biometrics allow people and machines to develop even more natural interactions, such as touch, image recognition, speaking, and body language. Currently it is primarily used in market research, but it also supports the selection of suitable competencies and human qualities (selecting the suitable workforce, choosing an expert). The role of AI is to process the huge amount of statistical data based on specified parameters (Kiss 2017).

Knowledge Development (Knowledge Creation)

The purpose of knowledge development is to ensure that employees of the company will generate the knowledge they need, including ideas, models, skills products, processes, and so on by choosing new or traditional methods of learning (training, e-learning, distance learning, school education) (Lovaszy 2017).

This purpose can be served well through follow-up that supports the application of AI solutions. The machine-based learning can have various forms (Hasznics and Nuridsány 2006). In the case of neural networks, a pattern-based learning is characteristic. The goal is to gain the appropriate knowledge from large amount of data and to change the behavior of a system through it (Watson's solutions).

Knowledge Sharing

Knowledge sharing is a critical phase of the knowledge management cycle and can be realized directly or indirectly. No matter how it is realized, people, organization, and technology are the key factors.

An important area related to AI is the expanding knowledge-sharing solution: a machine intellect is learning from other AI via the Internet. It is an easier way for machines to be taught the new assembly line process with this method than programming them one by one. The cooperative robots (cobots) were designed to work with people as their direct associates, preventing them from repetitive, burdensome, and dangerous operations. The cobots are connected to AI cloud applications, so they can be taught new work processes without programming (Tölgyes 2016; Kulaklia and Mahonyb 2014; Bíró 2017).

Preservation and Fixing of Knowledge

The main objective of knowledge preservation is to make the knowledge accumulated by the company accessible and ready to be utilized for many years. The explicit knowledge can be easily stored in an accessible form. A bigger problem for a company is retaining knowledge, which is hidden in the minds of employees. In the case of knowledge that is nonconvertible into an explicit form, organizational memory plays an important role.

This phase includes fixing of knowledge, systematization, storage, and update. These knowledge-based systems store the explicit form of knowledge of different problem areas or store expertise knowledge to handle a specific problem area. The inference systems are the catalysts of knowledge-based systems. For example, the central feature of case-based reasoning (CBR) is to solve the present problems based on the solutions of similar past problems (real situations and interpretations of them) (Ojala 2016; Stone et al. 2016). The system is capable of self-learning and is able to learn from experience if users provide feedback that solution offered was successful or not.

Use of Knowledge

The utilization of knowledge should ensure that knowledge is used productively and contributes to the improvement of the company performance (Fehér 2003).

Properly used knowledge is an integral part of the company's activity. The user-friendly nature of technology that makes knowledge accessible can help employees in the utilization of knowledge (i.e., using text-based AI for process efficiency), speed of problem solving, and enhancement on the quality of customer service (OTP Bank, Contact Center systems). Aside from intelligent search function, which can be applied in complex sentences or exact terms, the system is capable of proposing replies for e-mails and chat conversations and visualizing data sets or intelligence escalation, which can make certain processes more efficient (Hoeschl and Barcellos 2006; Hlács 2016).

Evaluation/Measurement of Knowledge

The last element of the model—reviewing the purpose of the process and knowledge—is usually not given the appropriate importance. The assessment and control of knowledge increase the visibility of the changes in organizational knowledge.

When evaluating the competitiveness of the organization, one must not forget that indicators measured in the traditional way will only partially show the real value of the company. Characteristics associated with human resources fall into the invisible category of the company's balance sheet. It would not be fair to dismiss them when evaluating the performance of the company, since the value of the organization is strongly associated with its employees and their ideas. The value of this invisible capital without humans is worthless or simply does not exist (Birzniece 2011; Neururer 2015).

Integrating AI—The Case-Based Reasoning

CBR is modeling the human thinking, which is a process of solving new problems based on the solutions of similar past problems and tasks by searching for and adopting documents from the past. It can be applied for the KMS in the following form. During the *knowledge identification* phase, the characteristic features describing similarities (codes) help to find the bearers of knowledge in the organization and through *knowledge acquisition* (if a new employee or expert is needed) find the staff to be recruited. It can identify the missing or outdated knowledge during the phase of *knowledge development.* During *knowledge sharing*, the solutions developed earlier are uploaded, and a predefined structure is applied and made available for use in the database later. A *knowledge store* is created, which makes available the previously tried and tested solutions, *utilizing knowledge* in the current case (Kiss 2017). The conditions to use the method efficiently are the following:

- Appropriate coding of cases
- Quick access to right solutions, tasks (qualities, competencies, etc.)
- Determining the degree of similarity

- Ensuring simple adaptation
- Constant update of the case-base

The CBR process is very simple. Individual cases are stored—together with the concrete solution of the cases—to create a case-base. When solving a new task/problem, the most similar case is selected from the case-base and the solution of the past case is adapted to the new one. Finally, the new results are added to the case-base (Badinszky 2008).

Representation of Cases

A problem to be solved during the development of an expert system based on CBR is the representation of cases.

A graph is used to describe the characteristics of the problem or task. The complexity of the graph depends on the complexity of the processes in the company and is prepared considering the characteristic features of the organization. A dialog (question-graph) will help the user to progress toward the solution of the problem, the code.

Identifying Similarity

The success of identifying similarity will fundamentally influence the success of the entire process and can therefore be considered as a key problem in the process. To solve this problem, an artificial neural network can be applied.

Artificial Neural Networks

Teaching is a prerequisite for the use of neural networks. Teaching patterns are used during the teaching process. These patterns include the primary similarity indexes and the final similarity indexes as well. This pattern is generated automatically using the case-base.

The Connection Between AI and the Building Blocks of KMS

Table 1.1 summarizes the steps of KMS, the processes (see above) required to implement them, and some examples of useful tools. Parallel with the

Table 1.1 Toolkits and relationship between KMS and AI

Digitalization areas		Artificial intelligence (AI) solutions (examples)
Probst's building blocks of KMS and their processes	Methodological background, management toolkit (examples)	
1.	Networking, decision models, brainstorming	OCR (optical character recognition), text production, deep learning, identity management, digital boardroom, probability networks, and so on
2.	Benchmarking, knowledge map, competency map, databases, data warehouses, document management systems	Machine learning (self-teaching system), content-based systematic search, intelligent response system, keyword recognition and self-reflection, big data solutions, cloud-based service
3.	Corporate records, learning, monitoring competitors, market information, Peer Assist, lessons learned, after-action review (AAR)	Text analysis, biometrics, chatbot, content-based semantic search, textmining, competitor intelligence (CI), translators, speech recognition (hidden Markov models), HR Hacking
4.	Learning, e-learning, training, brainstorming, talent programs, career plans, development programs, language learning, development of professional communities, Lifelong learning, blended learning	Follow-up systems, learner-teacher systems, chatbot, multi-agent intelligent tutoring system, MOOC (massive open online course), advisory artificial intelligence
5.	Knowledge sharing, on-the-job, video sharing, video conferencing, Wiki, World Café, storytelling, blogs, documentation systems, discussions, forums, brainstorming, ROCK (retention of critical knowledge), SharePoint, Yammer	Virtualization, speech recognition systems, text analysis, Google Docs, SharePoint, Social Learning, MyNet, GrapeVINE, intelligent escalation system, DeepCoder, case-based reasoning (CBR), artificial neural network, genetic algorithm, language translators, speech recognition (hidden Markov models), deep learning

(*Continued*)

Table 1.1 (Continued)

Digitalization areas		Artificial intelligence (AI) solutions (examples)
Probst's building blocks of KMS and their processes	Methodological background, management toolkit (examples)	
6.	Registers, work instructions, repositories, catalogs, printed and electronic forms, archive training and teaching materials	OCR, expert systems, Deep-Coder, knowledge-based system, CBR, interactive search engines, personal knowledge management, and content developing software
7.	AAR, retrospect, lessons learned, informal discussions, teamwork, big data	IoT (Internet of things), content management softwares, speech recognition softwares, intelligent response systems, cobots, virtualization, speech recognition (hidden Markov models)
8.	Analytical systems, measurement and management models, measurement decomposition structures	IoT, content management softwares, neural networks

digitalization areas, solutions are also presented supporting the most up-to-date solutions utilizing the possibilities provided by AI. The support provided by AI enables the attainment of a high level of knowledge organization and management that it can compete with human skills or exceed its boundaries in quality, quantity, and access to data and information. The AI solutions applied in each step and the basics of these solutions serve as examples that may change, develop, and multiply or in some cases disappear. It provides a framework for developers of KM systems and can contribute to the decision on the method to be applied (Mi az OCR Technológia 2017).

Conclusion

The potential of AI provides easily accessible tools for KMS. The development in this field is extremely fast and relies on the creativity of executives and how they can adapt to the processes that have been developed. A number of user-friendly and innovative solutions are available to the public and selecting the appropriate expertise is essential. This expertise will lead to the creation of tools not only for KMS but for other areas of organizational knowledge management as well. The self-learning feature of AI-based solutions should strengthen solutions and should be exploited as widely as possible. New frontiers of development should be considered.

The real challenge for everyone, not just IT specialists, is that the building blocks of KMS should form a real and viable system in the corporate practice. The AI solutions used to support the system should be integrated in each step to achieve a cooperation based on common principles, built on the same or similar logic, enabling them to be integrated into a workable system. Each of the steps presented cannot be explained without systematization. Most importantly, a solid framework for correlationships is essential.

References

Anklam, P., and S. Higgison. 2005. *The Social Network Toolkit: Building Organizational Performance through Collaborative Communities.* London: ARK Group.

Az öntanító AI. https://.groupmind.co/az-oentanito-ai

Badinszky, P. 2008. "BLOCKS—Személyes Tudásmenedzsment És Tartalomfejlesztő Szoftver." *Impresssum* 10, no. 6. http://ujsag.szie.hu/node/542

Barkovics, B. 2016. "Tisztázzuk az Ipar 4.0 alapfogalmait!" https://autopro.hu/trend/Tisztazzuk-az-Ipar-4-0-alapfogalmait/18073/

Bencsik, A. 2013. *Best Practice a Tudásmenedzsment Rendszer Kiépítésében.* London: Pearson.

Biró, K. 2017. "A Robotok és a Mesterséges Intelligencia Lendíthetik Fel a Japán Gazdaságot." https://sudy.co.hu/news/a-robotok-es-a-mesterseges-intelligencia-lendithetik-fel-a-japan-gazdasagot/

Birzniece, I. 2011. "Artificial Intelligence in Knowledge Management: Overview and Trends." *Scientific Journal of Riga* 46, pp. 5–11.

Chena, Y.-H., T.-P. Lina and D.C. Yen. 2014. "How to Facilitate Interorganizational Knowledge Sharing: The Impact of Trust." *Information & Management* 51, no. 5, pp. 568–78.

Davenport, T.H. 1996. "The Future of Knowledge Management." *CIO* 9, no. 5, pp. 30–31.

Davenport, T.H., and P. Laurence. 2001. "Tudásmenedzsment Budapest: Kossuth Kiadó."

Duhon, B. 1998. "It's All in our Heads." *Inform* 12, no. 8, pp. 8–13.

Fehér, P. 2003. "Tudásmenedzsment: A Jövő Szolgáltatása." In *Szolgáltatások a harmadik évezredben,* ed. P. Ilona, 417–62. Budapest: Aula.

Gholami, M.H., M.N. Asli, S. Nazari-Shirkouhi, and A. Noruzy. 2013. "Investigating the Influence of Knowledge Management Practices on Organizational Performance: An Empirical Study." *Acta Polytechnica Hungarica* 10, no. 2, pp. 205–13.

Hanako, A. 2016. *Artificial Intelligence and Knowledge Management.* U.S.: Willford Press.

Hasznics, M., and J. Nuridsány. 2006. "Hálózati Tudásmenedzsment Rendszerek Sajátosságai, Bevezetési Tapasztalatai." http://nws.niif.hu/ncd2006/docs/ahu/032.pdf

Hlács, F. 2016. "Együtt Kutatják a Mesterséges Intelligencia Hatásait a Tech-Óriások." *HWSW.* https://.hwsw.hu/hirek/56225/partnership-on-ai-mesterseges-intelligencia-google-ibm-amazon-microsoft.html

Hoeschl, H.C., and V. Barcellos. 2006. "Artificial Intelligence in Theory and Practice." In *IFIP 19th World Computer Congress International Federation for Information Processing, Volume 217,* ed. M. Bremer, 11–19. Boston: Springer.

Kiss, M. May 2017. "Tíz Eszköz, Ami Miatt a Mesterséges Intelligencia Nem Scifi, Hanem Inkább Szexi" *Forbes.* https://forbes.hu/legyel-jobb/tiz-eszkoz-ami-miatt-a-mesterseges-intelligencia-nem-scifi-hanem-inkabb-szexi/

Kulaklia, A., and S. Mahonyb. 2014. "Knowledge Creation and Sharing With Web 2.0 Tools for Teaching and Learning Roles in so-Called University 2.0." In *Procedia—Social and Behavioral Sciences 10th International Strategic Management Conference* 150, pp. 648–57.

Lovászy, L. June 2017. "A Mesterséges Intelligencia Egyes Kérdéseiről." *Világgazdaság.* https://.vg.hu/velemeny/mesterseges-intelligencia-egyes-kerdeseirol-532128/

Mi az OCR Technológia? 2017. https://ocrszoftver.hu/mi-az-ocr-technologia

"Mi is az a Mesterséges Intelligencia?—Mesterséges intelligencia II." 2012. *Infoter* Marc. http://infoter.blog.hu/2012/03/07/mi_is_az_a_mesterseges_intelligencia_mesterseges_intelligencia_ii

Neururer, M. 2015. "Artificial Intelligence in Knowledge Management." https://medium.com/artificial-intelligence-ai/the-role-of-artificial-intelligence-in-knowledge-management-309973209cfd

Nonaka, I., and H. Takeuchi. 1995. *The Knowledge-Creating Company: How Japanese Companies Create the Dynamics of Innovation.* New York, NY: Oxford University Press.

Ojala, M. 2016. "Best Practices in Cloud Solutions for the Enterprise." *KMWorld* 7/8, pp. 14–21.

Poór, J. 2010. *Menedzsment-Tanácsadási Kézikönyv.* Budapest: Akadémiai Kiadó.

Probst, G., S. Raub, and K. Romhardt. 2006. *Wissen Managen, Wie Unternehmen ihre Wertvollste Ressource Optimal Nutzen.* Wiesbaden: Gabler GmbH.

Stone, P., R. Brooks, R. Calo, and G. Hager. "Artificial Intelligence and Life in 2030." *One Hundred Year Study on Artificial Intelligence: Report of the 2015–2016 Study Panel.* Stanford, CA: Stanford University. http://ai100.stanford.edu/2016-report

Tölgyes, L. 2016. "A Mesterséges Intelligencia Kamaszkora". *IT Business,* Marc. http://.itbusiness.hu/Fooldal/rss_3/A_mesterseges_intelligencia_kamaszkora.html

CHAPTER 3

A New Perspective of Change for the Artificial Intelligence Age

Krishna Raj Bhandari

Introduction

With the accelerated pace of technological change triggered by artificial intelligence and cloud computing, the existing theories of change in developing and implementing strategy have fallen short. Not only are competitive landscapes changing, but products are also transforming the value chain. New business models are created and empowered by digitalization. In this new era, products are enabling the revolution by unlocking new value and transforming both companies and competition. The emergence of products and services enabled by digitalization moved several product and software firms from startup stages to mainstream organizations. However, models of change need to be augmented with relative mass flourishing, real option reasoning, and the CEO's attention. Also, leveraging contingencies with a positive mind-set is essential. This chapter proposes that relative mass flourishing, real option reasoning, and the CEO's attention together with leveraging contingencies are critical resources in the face of change to make the conversion process successful.

Human race is at the cusp of revolutionary change enabled by artificial intelligence (AI). This wave of change creates both opportunity and threat for the 21st century organizations. The opportunity is obvious as it enables new growth avenues, allows new business models, and creates competitive advantage. However, threat arises due to the pace of change and hastily done adaptation without proper thought process or solely based on hype. This is a grave concern in an AI economy since past hype is a present reality. Many firms are unprepared. The complexities are many: AI still lacks governance, is emerging too fast, and is unlike anything seen before.

According to Schildt (2016) in the age of AI, big data and complex algorithms are the cornerstone of software and can help do complex tasks such as driving cars. For sure, automation is one way of optimizing and building open systems. Algorithms pave the way for new approaches to *organize* work. Following Schildt (2016), this chapter touches upon optimizing-oriented and open-ended systems that benefit from big data and algorithmic management, which triggers a wave of change and transformation. In optimizing-oriented systems, the goal is to have algorithmic management of human work enabled by numerical data. However, in open-ended systems, the goal is to search for response to a wide range of managerial questions enabled by textual data or visualizations so that a new definition of tasks and resource allocation is possible. The wave of "computer assisted transparency" created by algorithm-processing conversations is possible but has advantages and disadvantages. Thus, nurturing advantages and minimizing disadvantages should be the goal of change management in the AI age.

According to Phelps (2013), the prosperity era in the history of capitalism was possible due to mass flourishing, a concept for mass innovation anchored in creativity, individualism, vitality, and self-expression. Though the history of capitalism illustrates this phenomenon, in the age of AI, the rationales seem different. Apple's app store-based business model captures the mass flourishing of developer community combined with Apple's corporatism, which resulted in a new level of dynamism in the mobile industry. The future of AI will enable such dynamism, which the author calls *relative mass flourishing*. The operational definition of the relative mass flourishing is the ratio of level of mass flourishing divided by the total sum effect of level of mass flourishing and level of corporatism. In this notion, the benefits arise from balancing the level of mass flourishing with a bit of corporatism.

According to Brynjolfsson (2013) the new machine age is "digital," "exponential," and "combinatorial." It drives abundance because the digitalization drives "almost" zero-marginal cost production and distribution. The innovation becomes "combinatorial" as previous products or platforms enable next generation of innovation. Even on its own, these trends are powerful. When they are combined, a wave of change emerges. The implications of this wave of change to business and society are so dramatic that it demands attention of the best minds that would be able to align and adapt to this new normal. Additional complication arises from the fact that the lessons acquired from the traditional software development are *not* easily transportable to machine-learning solutions. The best path is to race together with AI not against it. A key question is how should companies embrace change when little experience or history exists and uncertainty is high?

In the face of change and high uncertainty, the power of *experimentation and simulation* is one of the answers. Experimentation and simulation are excellent ways to feel one's way through when the rate of change is too fast to comprehend. However, for it to be effective and truly become part of the DNA of a firm, experimenting and simulations must become part of an operating philosophy of an organization. Hence, it should be led by the board and CEO with real option reasoning. Being a CEO will be challenging under these circumstances of massive change, as they would have to preserve the tradition while experimenting with the new. A method exists with which CEOs can do both. Such a method is presented in this chapter. There is a need for experimentation, learning, failing forward, and leveraging contingencies where CEO's attention and decision are critical resources.

The emergence of "smart, connected products" has transformed the competition. The products have become complex systems that combine hardware and software with cloud connectivity empowered by improvements in processing power and device miniaturization (Porter and Heppelmann 2014). Not only is the competitive landscape changing, but products are transforming the value chain and business models are growingly enabled by digitalization. Thus, digitalization is redefining industries and forcing companies to rethink everything they do throughout the value chain and even in the value networks. The changes are not only happening on the activities stream of the organization but there are profound implications for how work is organized such as cross-functional collaboration and creation of new functions. Though the change wave has just started, CEOs are required to focus their attention on this new emerging paradigm (Porter and Heppelmann 2015). A note of caution is that "smart, connected products" are not synonymous with the Internet of things (IoT). In the new era, products themselves are enabling the revolution by unlocking new value and transforming both companies and competition. Earlier waves of digitalization change were focused on value-chain automation and integration. The current paradigm is different as it embeds into products, creating added value and changing the locus of competition (Porter and Heppelman 2015).

The emergence of new wave of products and services enabled by the digitalization wave brought proven product and software development practice from the startup world to the mainstream organizations. A new movement called "Lean Startup" (Ries 2011) has been in the forefront of product development in the software industry. The core of this movement is to develop new products through "minimum viable"[1] development approach where a "build-measure-learn" loop is executed in a fast pace enabling experimentation and learning to avoid product failures in the long run. However, experimentation must be augmented by simulation to make sense in the algorithm-as-service business models in the age of AI.

In an environment where competitive dynamics are changing constantly, change is the new constant. Strategic management literature highlights dynamic capabilities in order to "sense," "seize," and "orchestrate" resources (Teece et al. 1997) and to gain a sustainable competitive advantage. However, as critically evaluated by Andreeva and Ritala (2016) there is a vacuum in understanding where these capabilities originate and how their dynamism lasts for a long time. Building further from the lean startup thinking, this chapter introduces the solution for the dilemma of origination of dynamic capabilities, called as "Lean Capability." Therefore, reasoning with the dynamic capability-based view (Teece et al. 1997;

---

[1] In this chapter, the word "product" is dropped from the "minimum viable product" (MVP) to make sense of seeking the right problem to solve rather than developing a product. This resonates very well with doing the "riskiest assumptions test" (RAT) (Higham 2016).

Teece 2007; Teece 2014), it is argued that "lean capability" anchored in the hypothesis-driven development where relative mass flourishing, CEO's attention, and real option reasoning as core elements are the new perspectives of change in the AI age. However, in this conceptualization "lean capability" goes beyond learning loops of lean startup thinking and encompasses Schildt's (2016) optimizing-oriented and open-ended systems where algorithm-as-service-based business models are possible for sustainable competitive advantage mainly driven by real option reasoning and attention as valuable, rare, inimitable, and nonsubstitutable resources (Barney 1991).

A New Perspective of Change

Combining hypothesis driven development (Taylor 2011; O'Reilly 2013) and the lean-startup thinking (Ries 2011) and arguments from Humble, Molesky, and O'Reilly (2014), the following new perspective of change for the AI age is proposed. In this framework, relative mass flourishing, CEO's attention (Ocasio 1997), and real option reasoning based on real option theory (ROT) (Trigeorgis and Reuer 2017) as the central elements and leveraging contingencies (Sarasvathy 2001) as a lever are the major contributions of this chapter. This chapter departs from all existing models that do not explicitly discuss the role of CEO's attention (Ocasio 1997) nor make real option reasoning as their reasoning instrument under the conditions of uncertainty or leverage contingencies for making a change project successful. The loop follows steps that are constantly moderated by rare resources—relative mass flourishing, CEO's attention, and real option reasoning.

McAfee, Brynjolfsson, Davenport, Patil, and Barton (2012) see big data as the next management revolution. Their argument is that big data enables better decisions by enabling evidence-based decision making but not on the intuition. This means today's concepts of decision making will change. For example, Google and Amazon benefitted from this revolution already but potential for other companies is equally good. However, if CEOs and senior managers do not adapt to the evidence-based decision making based on real option reasoning to build experimentation, learning, and optimizing culture, the new transformation will be challenging.

The role of data scientists in generating patterns and meaningful decision-making evidence is becoming crucial for the 21st century organizations. This change should reflect in the entire organization and a new meaning of "judgment" should be developed and contemplated.

Kolbjørnsrud, Kolbjørnsrud, Amico, Amico, Thomas, and Thomas (2017) argued that AI is becoming a cornerstone in transforming the nature of work and in creating a symbiosis of relationships among human beings and machines in organizations. However, managers are not ready. AI will change the reporting culture and nature of work itself. *This transformation is even larger than the industrial revolution.* Focusing only on managers to adjust to this new reality with their attention and real option reasoning-based thinking in the decision-making is not sufficient. To be successful in such a revolutionary change, top-level executives must empower society through relative mass flourishing.

(a) Relative mass flourishing, real option reasoning, and CEO's attention
(b) Observe
(c) Hypothesize
(d) Design experiment
(e) Identify the metric
(f) Conduct the experiment
(g) Evaluate or learn
(h) Decide
(i) Pivot
(j) Leveraging contingencies

In the following section, these phases of hypothesis regarding new theory of change as shown in Figure 3.2 are described.

Relative Mass Flourishing, Real Option Reasoning, and CEO's Attention

As discussed earlier the main thrust of this new perspective of change is to bring back the relative mass flourishing, real option reasoning, and CEO's attention at the center of discussion (see Figure 3.1 for a detailed real option reasoning approach and Figure 3.2 inside the hypothesis-driven

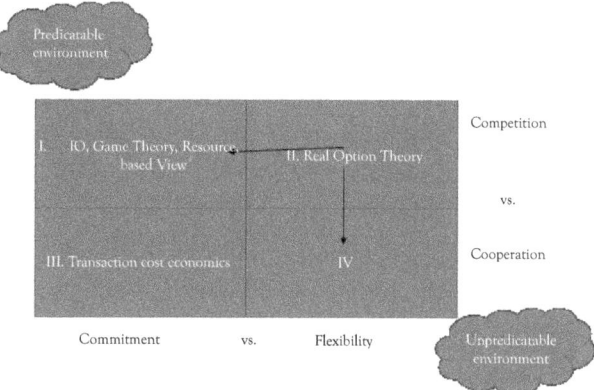

Figure 3.1 Real option reasoning (Adapted from Trigeorgis and Reuer (2017, p. 53) inspired by Trigeorgis and Baldi (2013))

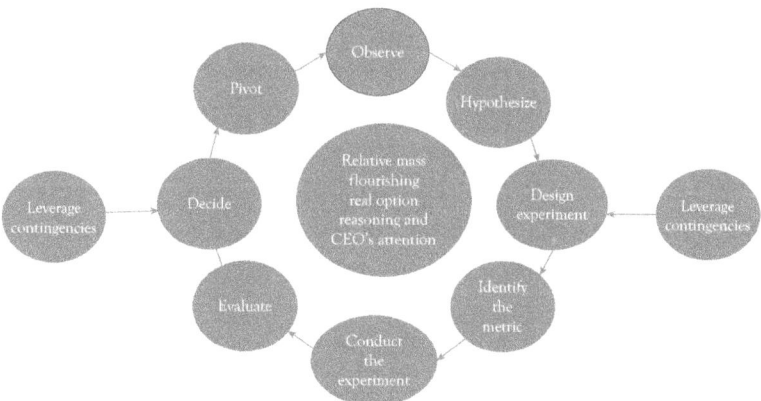

Figure 3.2 A new theory of change (Inspired by Phelps (2013); Ries (2011); and Humble et al. (2014)): Relative Mass Flourishing, Real Option Reasoning, and CEO's Attention

learning, optimizing loop). Balancing the need for a new business model where mass flourishing is possible and at the same time an optimum level of corporatism is utilized would be the CEO's agenda as Apple did through App Store. However, without the attention by the CEO and in the absence of real option reasoning, change projects aiming for mass flourishing will fail. These three elements become the DNA of companies in the AI age to run fast experiments to learn, adapt, and optimize. Also, as evident from the model, the current reality is that information technology is not only a function anymore. It pervades and changes the business model and hence changes the business strategy completely.

The creation and implementation of strategy are normally top-down but in current reality bottom-up approaches are needed. Thus, the CEO's attention is even crucial so that he does not miss the boat of change. In real option reasoning, being competitive and flexible at the same time is a trade-off and CEO's role in brokering this balance is crucial as shown in quadrant II in Figure 3.1. The focus of the organization should go beyond learning loops to optimizing loops enabled by machine learning and algorithm-based programming.

Observe

The first step in the loop is to gather information, observe patterns, and make sense of the current operating environment and the business itself. Most of the time executives are not alert on what is happening. While observing, the CEO's attention overload deters them from focusing on the right change loop. To avoid attention overload, multiple but quick loops must be done. The loop that validates hypothesis must be pursued and the others must be discarded. However, the goal is to enable relative mass flourishing with algorithm-as-service business model.

Hypothesize

Most of the change management processes are without proper hypothesis to test and learn from. Therefore, once the operating environment and business itself are observed in step "A," a plausible hypothesis to test and learn from should be developed. The hypothesis development as other processes needs to be verified by the CEO, anchored in real option reasoning and furthering relative mass flourishing.

Design Experiment

This is the very minimum viable experiment with limited resources to test the hypothesis and learn from. Not only the organizational resources but also the CEO's attention as a resource are scarce and need to be managed well. Therefore, rather than developing a full product or service, the idea is to build a prototype or a smaller version of the test item to test the hypothesis on the riskiest assumptions and understand the numbers behind the test.

Identify the Metric

The goal of the experiment is to measure progress. One needs to define actionable metrics (not the vanity metrics) for the hypothesis testing. If a right metric is not in place, possibility of learning will be missed. Therefore, it is very important to set the metrics in the design phase already.

Conduct the Experiment

Once the metrics are identified, the next step is to conduct the experiment. For sure, CEO's attention is needed in this phase as well as it was needed for the other phases. The goal is to fail safe and fail fast. The culture in the organization must embrace these initiatives. Otherwise it will not succeed.

Evaluate/Learn

As mentioned in the start of the experiment, the goal is to have a validated learning as a measure of progress as suggested by Ries (2011). Therefore, after the experiment, there is a need to make sense of the metrics being tracked. This phase is crucial in making the next move.

Decide Through Real Option Reasoning

Though real option reasoning to balance competitive moves with flexibility is always there, this is a particular phase where, once the hypothesis is proven right, one must decide to go further in evangelizing the change program. If not, the next phase of "pivot" needs to be executed to go through the change loop once again. Leveraging contingencies are a rare resource in the face of uncertainty and at this stage pausing and digesting the numbers to nurture intuition are highly recommended. As the decision making under uncertainty is hard, the strategic management literature suggests that ROT (Trigeorgis and Reuer 2017) is a good solution as shown in Figure 3.1 earlier. Quadrant II is important because the strategic dilemma of competition versus cooperation is high and at the same time commitment versus flexibility dimension is also high. The nature of change in the AI age is uncertain and betting on only one option is not preferred.

Pivot

If the decision in the previous step shows that the minimum viable experiment did not satisfy the need, then the next loop needs to be initiated with a new set of hypotheses. This is called pivot by Ries (2011). The "pivot" can take us to new sets of hypotheses and tests. Or this "pivot" becomes a new scalable solution for customer creation and company building (Blank 2013).

Leveraging Contingencies

Upon reflection from the effectuation theory (Sarasvathy 2001), in entrepreneurial opportunity creation the role of contingencies is central. Those who would like to manage well in the face of uncertainty, those entrepreneurial managers need to be able to leverage contingencies (both internal and external) to become successful. In articulating this phenomenon, while designing experiments or at the final decision point, reflecting on the role of contingencies is wildly important. This becomes a rare resource while operating under extreme uncertainty as is the attention.

Discussions: Revisiting Porter, Barney, Phelps, and Teece

As discussed earlier, relative mass flourishing is measured as the ratio between the level of mass flourishing divided by the total sum effect of level of mass flourishing and corporatism. In this conceptualization, mass flourishing at the expense of corporatism will not result into economies of scale nor economies of scope. This chapter goes a step further on the Phelps (2013) conceptualization of mass flourishing and creates an index on balancing mass flourishing with corporatism. Too little of it or too much of it does not lead to an optimum level of firm performance. One example is how Apple has developed a developer community with a business model anchored in the App Store. This is a form of mass flourishing and dynamism in the developer community but combined with the corporatism of Apple as an orchestrator. With the advent of AI, such business models could be scaled and nurtured well. However, as shown in Figure 3.3, at low level of AI the curve shows lower performance but at high level of AI the performance curve shifts to the next level. This simulation suggests that while balancing mass flourishing and corporatism are needed but at the same time level of AI needs to be assessed. However, the pattern of too much or too little of anything is detrimental to performance is valid even in the presence of AI or absence of it for that matter.

What would the key strategic management discourse offer about this phenomenon and new perspective of change? Looking from the lens of Porter, he is not ready to change his old economics-based thinking as demonstrated by the latest papers on the impact of information technology on the value chain and strategy. Similarly, Barney's thinking has not evolved since 1991 except it has been labeled as tautological by some authors. Teece has ventured into theory of the multinationals in his 2014 publication. But looking from the dynamic capabilities standpoint (Teece et al. 1997; Teece 2007) one can feel that there are elements of *sense, seize, configure* emerging into new models albeit with a new purpose.

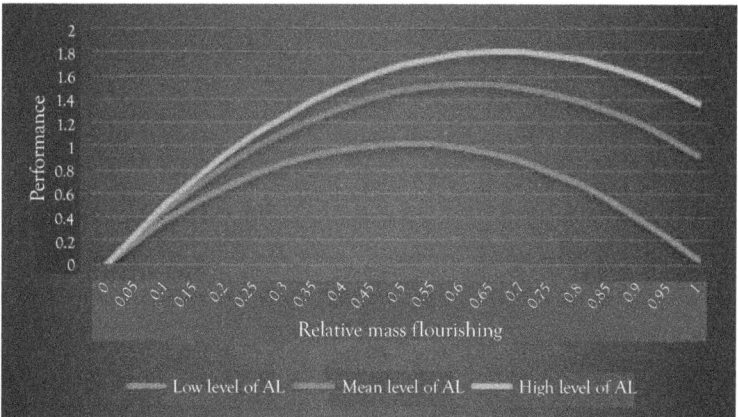

Figure 3.3 Impact of level of artificial intelligence on the curvilinear relationship between relative mass flourishing and firm performance

Thus, this chapter highlights the need for a new perspective of change as a process that managers and policy makers alike can take in building the 21st century organization. However, the addition to this debate are the core circle of relative mass flourishing, real option reasoning, CEO's attention, and leveraging contingencies. CEOs have limited attention capacity and they need to *sense, seize, and reconfigure* the resources properly in a fast experimentation and learning cycles so that old planning school does not become a bottleneck for the implementation of change.

Based on the discussion above, there are seven key managerial implications:

- Focus on relative mass flourishing, real option reasoning, and CEO's attention.
- Drive the experimentation culture, reward failure, and celebrate learning.
- Build validated learning as a tool for measuring progress rather than existing accounting metrics.
- Find early change agents, nurture them, and use them as ambassadors of change.
- Give managers ownership and control to create and manage projects.
- Leverage contingencies and return on luck.
- Follow open innovation and open strategizing.

Policy Implications

This chapter has followed in the footsteps of practitioners and academicians alike to assert that the new artificial wave driven by "digital," "exponential," and "combinatorial" trend is faced with dilemmas. On the one hand productivity is rising but on the other hand the employment is falling (Brynjolfsson 2013). This is the most alarming "great decoupling" in history. There is a race between people and machines. And the machines are winning that race. The discussions in this chapter, thus, further the notion suggested by Brynjolfsson (2013) that policy makers must think to race *with* the machines not *against* the machines. In this symbiosis of man and machine no supercomputer can beat teamwork.

References

Andreeva, T., and P. Ritala. 2016. "What are the Sources of Capability Dynamism? Reconceptualizing Dynamic Capabilities From the Perspective of Organizational Change." *Baltic Journal of Management* 11, no. 3, pp. 238–59.

Barney, J. 1991. "Firm Resources and Sustained Competitive Advantage." *Journal of Management* 17, no. 1, pp. 99–120.

Blank, S. 2013. "Why the Lean Start-up Changes Everything?" *Harvard Business Review* 91, no. 5, pp. 63–72.

Brynjolfsson, E. 2013. "The Key to Growth? Race with the Machines." https://. ted.com/talks/erik_brynjolfsson_the_key_to_growth_race_em_with_em_ the_machines#t-269127 (accessed March 09, 2017).

Higham, R. 2016. "The MVP is Dead. Long live the RAT." https://hackernoon. com/the-mvp-is-dead-long-live-the-rat-233d5d16ab02#.x9gpchhne (accessed March 08, 2017).

Humble, J., J. Molesky, and B. O'Reilly. 2014. *Lean Enterprise: How High Performance Organizations Innovate at Scale*. Boston, MA: O'Reilly Media, Inc.

Kahneman, D. 2011. *Thinking, Fast and Slow*. Macmillan. London, UK

Kolbjørnsrud, V., V. Kolbjørnsrud, R. Amico, R. Amico, R.J. Thomas, and R.J. Thomas, 2017. "Partnering with AI: How Organizations Can Win Over Skeptical Managers." *Strategy & Leadership* 45, no. 1, pp. 37–43.

McAfee, A., E. Brynjolfsson, T.H. Davenport, D.J. Patil, and D. Barton. 2012. "Big Data: The Management Revolution." *Harvard Business Review* 90, no. 10, pp. 61–67.

O'Reilly. 2013. "How to Implement Hypothesis-driven Development." https:// barryoreilly.com/2013/10/21/how-to-implement-hypothesis-driven- development/ (accessed March 02, 2017).

Phelps, E.S. 2013. *Mass Flourishing: How Grassroots Innovation Created Jobs, Challenge, and Change*. Princeton, New Jersey, US: Princeton University Press.

Porter, M.E., and J.E. Heppelmann. 2014. "How Smart, Connected Products are Transforming Competition." *Harvard Business Review* 92, no. 11, pp. 64–88.

Porter, M.E., and J.E Heppelmann. 2015. "How Smart, Connected Products are Transforming Companies." *Harvard Business Review* 93, no. 10, pp. 96–114.

Power, B. 2014. "How GE Applies Lean Startup Practices." *Harvard Business Review* (accessed April 23, 2014).

Power, B. 2014. "How Watson Changed IBM." https://hbr.org/2014/08/how- watson-changed-ibm (accessed March 13, 2017).

Ries, E. 2011. *The Lean Startup: How Today's Entrepreneurs Use Continuous Innovation to Create Radically Successful Businesses*. New York, NY: Crown Business.

Sarasvathy, S.D. 2001. "Causation and Effectuation: Toward a Theoretical Shift from Economic Inevitability to Entrepreneurial Contingency." *Academy of Management Review* 26, no. 2, pp. 243–63.

Schildt, H. 2017. "Big Data and Organizational Design–the Brave New World of Algorithmic Management and Computer augmented Transparency." *Innovation* 19, no. 1, pp. 1–8.

Taylor, J.L. 2011. "Hypothesis Driven Development." http://drdobbs.com/architecture-and-design/hypothesis-driven-development/229000656 (accessed March 02, 2017).

Teece, D.J., G. Pisano, and V. Shuen. 1997. "Dynamic Capabilities and Strategic Management." *Strategic Management Journal,* pp. 509–33.

Teece, D.J. 2007. "Explicating Dynamic Capabilities: The Nature and Microfoundations of (Sustainable) Enterprise Performance." *Strategic Management Journal* 28, no. 13, pp. 1319–50.

Trigeorgis, L., and F. Baldi. 2013. "Patent Strategies: Fight or Cooperate?" In *Real Options Annual Conference.* http://realoptions. org/openconf2013/data/papers/45.pdf (accessed June 2014).

Trigeorgis, L., and J.J. Reuer. 2017. "Real Options Theory in Strategic Management." *Strategic Management Journal* 38, no. 1, pp. 42–63.

CHAPTER 4

Artificial Intelligence in Strategic Human Resources Management

Al Naqvi

Introduction: The Rise of the Cognitive Era

The rise of artificial intelligence (AI) in business is expected to have a profound impact on human resources management. The change will include both how the HR function is managed and approached (HR management) by companies, and how the function is practiced (HR practice). Since the advent of AI implies that machines will compete with human work, human and organizational transformation is at the core of the change. Strategic human resource management (SHRM) focuses on organizational performance and, in the new cognitive era, the practice of SHRM will undergo major changes. Both aspects of human resource management—HR practice and HR management—are discussed in light of the upcoming cognitive era.

When it comes to AI, human resources departments need to make the following two assessments:

1. How will the advent of AI improve the function of human resources management (HRM)?
2. How would the dawn of AI change the responsibility, function, and role of human resources?

The first assessment can be restated as a concern or inquiry into what technologies and systems can be used to manage and improve the existing functions of human resources. With the new cognitive technologies coming out, this will become a constant struggle to select, adopt, and implement new technologies.

The second reflects on how human resources will need to realign, reinvent, and reshape itself as a function for the new era of AI. This implies that expected changes will be structurally significant and therefore their impact will be broad and deep.

In this chapter, both issues are covered. The terms cognitive era, cognitive revolution, and AI will be used interchangeably.

The word "rise" is meant to signify the following: (a) the AI technology has matured; (b) AI is being applied in products and services; (c) AI is capable of creating and sustaining competitive advantage for companies; (d) AI is expected to have a significant impact on the economy; and (e) AI is something that executives and professionals should pay attention to.

Since the term AI was coined in 1956 at a conference at Dartmouth, the AI field struggled to become mainstream and gain wide acceptance (Chen et al. 2016). The unfortunate cycle of Optimism > Invest > Disappointment > Pessimism got repeated at least three times and is known as the winters of AI. In the down periods, investment dried out and even government pulled funding from research. More recently, however, the field has rematerialized as a formidable and powerful force and its reemergence is being considered as permanent and sustainable. Specifically, improvements in four factors, processing power, algorithms, data management, and global connectivity, have set the irreversible course of AI (Naqvi 2017a). Understandably, in the last few years the field has received significant attention and significant investment is flowing into the field (White House 2016).

While the technology is being applied in almost all industries and functions, its impact on the human resources function is particularly important. First, human resources departments focus on "humans" and clearly the advent of AI poses a clear challenge to the skill set, competence, and capability of humans. Second, human resources plays a major role in the overall strategy of a firm and as such it is important to understand the impact of AI.

What makes AI different and far more powerful than any other technology we have ever experienced as civilization is that it is "cognitive."

In other words, unlike machines that can only respond to human command and that have no mind of their own, AI-based machines will and do have the ability to learn, adapt, make decisions, accumulate experience, and even take actions as humans do (Naqvi 2017b). These machines go beyond the physical work automation and can now automate mental or cognitive functions performed by humans.

While the potential and future of such machines can force us to draw out numerous scenarios that can include the rise of killer robots to a world run by AI, for the purposes of this chapter we will focus on the technologies that are currently available, in the works, or whose induction can be reasonably foreseen in the next five-year period.

The HR Management: Realigning the Department

Human resources management is a vibrant and fast-developing field. SHRM is considered as a subfield of HRM. The word "strategic" in SHRM signifies that it focuses on organizational performance and not on individual performance and that human resources systems are approached as part of solving the broader business problems (Becker and Huselid 2006). Becker and Huselid argued that the way human resources contributes to the competitive advantage of a firm is when HR architecture is aligned with the strategic capabilities and business processes of a firm. To create that alignment, one of the specific configurations stems from the five-P model of human resources (philosophy, policies, programs, practices, and processes) whereby the five elements are systematically linked with the strategic needs of the firm (Schuler 1992). Schuler explains that the strategic needs reflect management's overall plan for survival, growth, adaptability, and profitability.

SHRM can be approached from many theoretical angles (Wright and McMahan 1992) and it is well established that the function is strategic and its practitioners need to make sure that it is approached strategically. Additionally, modern developments clarify that the focus on the internal resources rather than the external perspective (e.g., industry structure and so on) is becoming a greater source of competitive advantage and leading to a convergence between SHRM and strategy of a firm (Wright et al. 2001).

Thus, the AI systems for SHRM need to be approached from the perspective of creating competitive advantage for a firm. As such, the top alignment of SHRM AI infrastructure needs to be such that the architectural layer captures the strategy of the firm. Given that the competitive dynamics of the cognitive era are different than the old era of industrial and information age, it is important to establish that link between the firm strategy and its human resources systems. Beyond the core strategic link, the functional aspects of human resources cannot be ignored.

One of the powerful aspects of SHRM is that it focuses on the organizational performance and the individual performance is aligned with the overall firm's performance. In that regard, the cognitive era technology plays a key role in connecting and clarifying the organizational strategy and constantly aligns it with the functional aspects of HRM. This means that the new model offers an incredible opportunity to link organizational goals with employee goals and to be able to manage them at a very detailed level. As the organizational goals change, they are rapidly reflected in the individual performance goals.

From the functional aspects of HRM, we know that factors such as recruitment, retention, development, staffing, benefits management, and so on are important aspects of running a human resources department. In fact, from the cognitive capability perspective one can think of HRM as a function that automates human work and provides information. Using this simple framework, Strohmeier and Piazza developed a model that integrated the automated and information capabilities with the functional aspects of staffing, performance management, development, and compensation (Strohmeier and Piazza 2015). Defining the major AI techniques as knowledge-related techniques, thought-related techniques, and language-related techniques, they proposed a conceptual architecture for the cognitive era human resources.

Developing the above further, we can study HRM from the aspects of the SADAL® framework. The SADAL® framework explains the capabilities of cognitive systems and SADAL is an acronym for sense, analyze, decide, act, and learn. Specifically, it implies that the cognitive technologies can use these five elements to interact with and influence their environment. When applied in the HR frameworks, one can take the major processes or the functional areas and determine what would constitute as the SADAL® features. For example, recruitment is an expensive and time-consuming process that requires significant amount of human effort. When SADAL framework is applied, one can determine the following about the recruitment process.

The important questions are: What sensors will be needed to screen the information embedded in the environment? How will that information be analyzed? What will be the decision trigger points and how will those decisions be made? What will be the actions taken once decisions are made? What experiences will accumulate and what learning will take place in the software agent?

For example, recruitment is triggered by the resource needs of an organization. That need can arise as a new position is created or due to an existing vacancy. An existing vacancy can happen because someone left the firm, got fired, got promoted, or changed jobs internally. Software agents can be designed to not only quickly identify such vacancies but also project based upon existing data. The process of sensing and analyzing thus involves both identifying and determining based upon given information but also projecting or predicting. For example, a software program can predict that a vacancy will be created in a certain department due to retention failure and therefore it can preemptively plan for filling that vacancy. This implies that the agent was able to determine and predict the retention failure. This retention failure could have been detected based upon the historical data acquired from the firm. Using various features the system could have determined that the current employee will leave within four months and therefore a decision will be triggered to determine if the search for a replacement should begin now. At the very least, the system will be able to identify potential candidates to fill the job both internally and externally.

The recruitment agent will do the search and bring data back for the HR to make sure that ideal candidates are preemptively identified. In addition to bringing the resume, the agent can also provide relevant information about the prospective candidate that can be used to configure the package or even the interview for the candidate such that it increases the likelihood of the candidate accepting the job. For example, assuming that the candidate is considered fit for the job and the firm is trying to land the candidate, if the data shows that the candidate is motivated by environmental and sustainability issues of the world, having the head of environmental management of the firm interview the candidate would be a better idea instead of the head of legal affairs. That way, the candidate may get attracted to the environmental commitment and record of the firm and hence the likelihood of landing the candidate can be increased significantly. Could such use of information be considered invasion of privacy is a topic that will require a separate analysis, however the discussion is active and hotly debated (Captain 2016).

Similarly, many types of cognitive use cases can be designed and processes automated. For example, there is notable impact on performance evaluation (Gürbüz and Albayrak 2014).

The HR Practice: Reinventing the Profession

The second challenge for assessment was to understand how to realign, reshape, and reinvent the profession. The underlying reason for this part of the challenge is that the AI change is no ordinary change. Technological changes tend to impact the core structures of the economy and cause major shifts (Perez 2002). Nothing remains as before and the same is true for departments and functions.

For the HR function the following will be relevant and timely: (1) understanding the strategy of the firm; (2) developing a machine-human scenario; (3) developing a strategic transformation plan; (4) evaluating the performance requirements and incentives; (5) development; and (6) developing an ethics framework.

The starting point is understanding the strategy of the firm. While it can be argued that SHRM, by definition, focuses on the strategy of a firm and hence why is it important to repeat this requirement in practice management? The important distinction here is that this aspect of a firm's strategy includes its cognitive transformation strategy (Holtel 2016) and not just any strategy. Holtel argues that just as steam engine's invention created an immense, unprecedented, and often unpredictable change, the advent of AI will do the same. In this cognitive transformation, the company switches to an entirely new way of doing things, reinventing its core processes, and carefully allocating them between humans and machines. This is no easy task.

This work will require a detailed analysis of how the strategy of a firm will be manifested in its various departments and how the needs of the departments will change. This means that the HR professionals would need to develop a keen and powerful understanding of each and every function and its emerging needs. Thus, the plan for HR will be tightly integrated with the plans of all other functions since the uncertainty prevalent in other functions will impact the HR plans. The HR function would need to keep immense flexibility in its operation.

Developing a Machine-Human Scenario: HR departments are well equipped to develop resource requirement plans for humans—but now they would need to develop scenarios that will include the machine-human plans. This implies that the human-machine interaction should be considered when designing work processes. The human-machine interaction will impact not only incentive plans and motivation, but also self-esteem and dignity of a human being. The human-machine scenarios also imply that HR would need to determine plans for retraining employees, reallocating them to other jobs, or laying off. In simplest terms, HR departments would need to recognize that they are now responsible for managing two types of work resources: human and machine.

Developing a Strategic Transformation Plan: From an internal firm perspective, the cognitive transformation is centered upon human augmentation or replacement. Thus, the cognitive transformation will mostly be about, and relevant to, the human resource and hence HR departments will be fundamental to driving and leading the change.

Evaluating the Performance Requirements and Incentives: One of the greatest contributions and challenges of the HR departments will be developing performance expectations and incentive systems for human employees. The problem with defining the performance expectations will be that, as soon as performance expectations are defined, they will become a moving target since machines will be competing for human work. This scenario implies that incentive plans would need to be flexible.

Development: HR departments will have new and perhaps never-seen-before responsibilities to develop human employees. The upcoming cognitive revolution has placed, and will continue to do so, such an immense pressure on human workers that employees will have to constantly reinvent themselves. This reinvention implies that HR departments would need to help orchestrate training programs. Some companies have chief learning officers and others do not. In both cases, HR departments will need to help develop employee transformation programs—which may include significant retraining.

Ethics: One of the most important challenges that human resources will need to incorporate will be that the departments will be required to constantly reevaluate and reassess ethics. John Summer has pointed out some very interesting issues (Summer 2017), including:

- Who owns the employee data?
- How do you disagree with computer decision?
- What is the liability of human decisions?
- How to tell the difference between manipulation and motivation?

The reason ethical question will constantly challenge employers is systems will continue to evolve and learn. Organizations will be confronted with new ethical dilemmas and HR departments will need to constantly enhance and adjust to these challenges.

Commentary

Human resources is about managing organizational performance. Organizations experience and manage change but in the process dynamically change themselves (Tsoukas and Chia 2002). Organizations also evolve and can be viewed as complex adaptive systems (Dooley 1997). As the article shows, companies will be confronted with significant change. The future is both complex and at times unpredictable. What makes this change different is not only the fact that it will display characteristics of major technological transformation; it will force companies to adapt quickly. Competitive advantage in an environment like that is a moving target, often short-lived, and subject to constant revision. Competition emerges from unexpected areas and in ways that are hard to imagine. For example, tech firms like Google have interest in entering the auto sector and Amazon acquired a grocery chain Whole Foods.

HR departments need to be open to change and prepared for leading it. Leading change in this respect implies that HR leaders would need to reequip their departments with powerful new technologies while simultaneously redesigning and realigning their functions to the new challenges.

Humans have never encountered a situation in which they had to compete with a cognitive technology. This technology is different. It is a thinking machine and it is designed to learn. No other department will have a greater challenge than the HR department.

References

Becker, B.E., and M.A. Huselid. 2006. "Strategic Human Resources Management : Where Do We Go From Here?" *Journal of Management* [Online], pp. 32898–925.

Captain, S. 2016. "Not-so-human Resources." *Fast Company* (October), p. 44.

Chen, N., L. Christensen, K. Gallagher, R. Mate, and G. Rafert. 2016. *Global Economic Impacts Associated with Artificial Intelligence Nicholas* [online], available from http://.analysisgroup.com/uploadedfiles/content/insights/publishing/ag_full_report_economic_impact_of_ai.pdf [online]. available from http://.analysisgroup.com/uploadedfiles/content/insights/publishing/ag_full_report_economic_impact_of_ai.pdf

Dooley, K.J. 1997. "A Complex Adaptive Systems Model of Organization Change." *Nonlinear dynamics, psychology, and life sciences* 1, no. 1 [Online], pp. 69–97.

Gürbüz, T., and Y.E. Albayrak. 2014. "An Engineering Approach to Human Resources Performance Evaluation : Hybrid MCDM Application With Interactions." *Applied Soft Computing Journal* [Online], 21365–375. [online], available from http://dx.doi.org/10.1016/j.asoc.2014.03.025

Holtel, S. 2016. "Artificial Intelligence Creates a Wicked Problem for the Enterprise." *Procedia–Procedia Computer Science* [Online], pp. 99171–80.

Naqvi, A. 2017a. *Chapter in Global Business Intelligence*. In ed. M. Munoz. New York, NY: Routledge.

Naqvi, A. 2017b. "Competitive Dynamics of Artificial Intelligence Economy: The Wicked Problem of Cognitive Competition." *Journal of Economics Library* 4, no. 2, pp. 187–93.

Perez, C. 2002. *Technological Revolutions and Financial Capital: The Dynamics of Bubbles and Golden Ages*. Northampton, MA: Edward Elgar.

Schuler, R.S. 1992. "Strategic Human Resources Management : Linking the People with the Strategic Needs of the Business." *Organizational Dynamics* 21, no. 1, pp. 18–32.

Strohmeier, S., and F. Piazza. 2015. *Chapter 7 Artificial Intelligence Techniques in Human Resource Management—A Conceptual Exploration in Book: Intelligent Techniques in Engineering Management*. In eds. C. Kahraman and S.Ç. Onar. New York, NY :Springer.

Summer, J. 2017. "Artificial Intelligence: Ethics, Liability, Ownership and HR." *Workforce Solutions Review*, pp. 24–26.

Tsoukas, H., and R. Chia. 2002. "On Organizational Becoming: Rethinking Organizational Change." *Organization Science* [Online], 13 (October 2015), pp. 567–82.

White House. 2016. *Preparing for the future of Artificial Intelligence* [online], available from https://obamawhitehouse.archives.gov/sites/default/files/white house_files/microsites/ostp/NSTC/preparing_for_the_future_of_ai.pdf

Wright, P.M., and G. McMahan. 1992. "Theoretical Perspectives for Strategic Human Resource Management." *Journal of Management* 18, no. 2, pp. 295–320.

Wright, P.M., B.B. Dunford, S.A. Snell. 2001. *Human Resources and the Resource Based View of the Firm*. pp. 27701–21.

CHAPTER 5

Artificial Intelligence and Cybersecurity

Mehrdad Sharbaf

Information systems are greatly identified as the engine that drives and supports the U.S. and global economy, giving industry a strategic competitive advantage in global markets, enabling the federal government and agencies to collaborate among themselves, and building a 21st century digital government platform to provide better services to their citizens. The 21st century is the age of digital information when information within corporation becomes an imperative important strategically and, it is valuable resource than ever as the development of such field like business economics intelligent underlines it. But information systems are exposed to serious internal and external threats that can have adverse effects on organizational operations. Unfortunately, the complexity of security attacks, and increased number of vulnerabilities, and lack of effectively protecting against the dynamically evolving attacks within organization networks have greatly increased over the past few years, even the best security mechanisms can be bypassed by professional hackers. The National Institute of Standards and Technology's (NIST) National Vulnerability Database (NVD), established just a little over a year ago, now contains information on 20,000 computer system vulnerabilities, up from the original 12,000, and the website receives hits at a rate of 25 million per year. For those organizations trying to prevent computer system attacks, keeping up with the hundreds of new vulnerabilities discovered each month can be an overwhelming and challenging task (http://nvd.nist.gov/). In the recent research survey, it shows (Figure 5.1) the

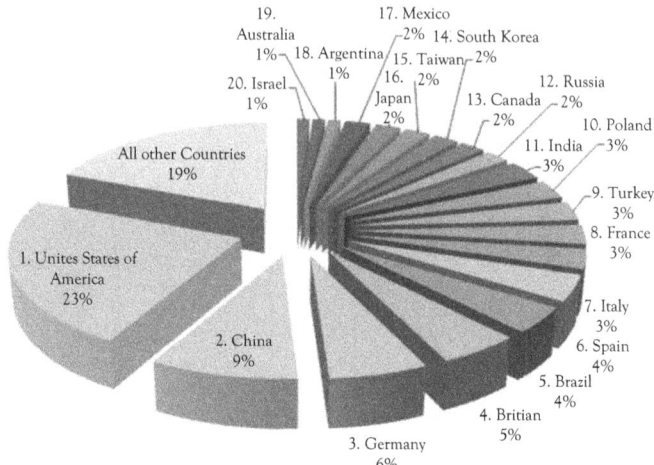

Cybercrime: Top 20 countries

Figure 5.1 Countries by Cyber-attack

United States having by far the most cyber-attacks, followed by China and then Germany.

Countries by Cyber-Attack

Despite widespread training, education, and awareness of the impact of cybercrime, cyber-attacks continue to occur frequently and result in serious financial consequences for businesses and government institutions. This statistic gives information on the percentage of annualized cybercrime cost of the U.S. companies in 2015, by type of attack. During that year, 24 percent of costs caused by cybercrime were due to malicious code (Figure 5.2) (http://.statista.com/statistics/193431/annual-cyber-crime-cost-for-us-companies-by-attack-type/).

Ponemon Institute's 2015 cybercrime study report found that the cost of digital crime rose by 19 percent in the last year, and the average annual loss to companies worldwide is 47.7 million.

Many organizations are still applying manual efforts to compose cybersecurity threat findings and to characterize them with external threat information. Using these mechanisms, it can be time consuming to detect,

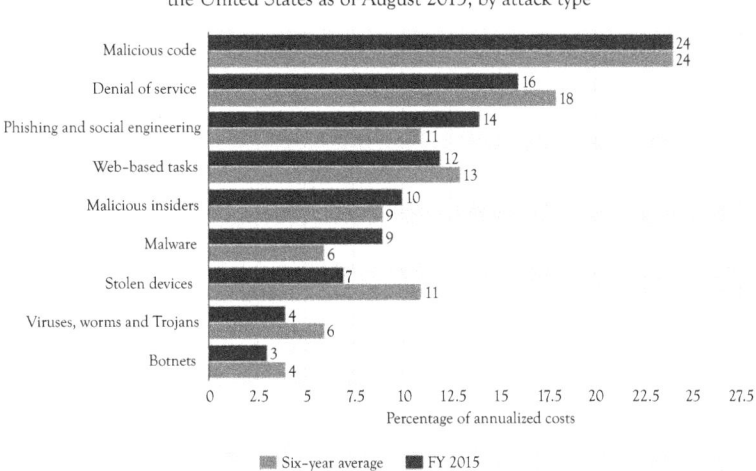

Figure 5.2 The percentage of annualized cybercrime cost of the U.S. companies in 2015

and identify intrusions, during which time intruders can exploit vulnerabilities to compromise systems, and extract sensitive organization information. To address these issues, and challenges, organizations are making progress toward better condition in cybersecurity by applying artificial intelligence (AI) in their business operation. AI offers enormous potential to enable more efficient and effective business and government operations. AI can help an organization to predict, prevent, and defeat attacks. For example, product recommendations from services such as Amazon and Netflix that evolve through users' web experiences are powered by machine learning, or digital images from millions of satellite observations can be analyzed for environmental or socioeconomic trends using machine learning to identify patterns of change and development, by applying neural networks, genetic algorithms, Markov models of various sorts, and other machine learning to detect anomalies to packet streams, protocol uses patterns. This chapter creates and develops a new perspective in information security management, and it introduces a new concept called AI and cybersecurity. It supports the organization cybersecurity strategy in their information security management processes by applying the AI techniques. This chapter also discusses about managing information security by applying AI in organization cybersecurity operation, and businesses can strategize how to implement AI within their organization. Also, the latest AI products related to cybersecurity will be discussed.

Given the increased dependence of businesses on computer-based systems and networks, vulnerabilities of systems abound, lack of cyber security strategies, lack of proper commitment from top management, lack of proper policies, standard, awareness, and education. For that reason over the past decades managing the information systems security has risen to be a challenging task. Clearly, exclusive reliance on either the technical or the managerial controls is inadequate. Rather, a new perspective to information security approach is needed. Technical approaches by itself cannot work out an answer or solution for the security problems for a simple reason that information security is not merely a technical problem, but also is a management problem.

A core concept and message is that good security in an organization starts at the top management, not with technical tools such as firewalls, intrusion detection systems, antivirus, or biometrics devices. Top senior management has a much more significant role to play in achieving security than they may think.

The first strategy of organization must be to develop and monitor mechanism to evaluate the quality of information security by applying the AI techniques to secure information in enterprise.

The development of evaluation mechanism depends on the risk assessment of the organization. The organization shall specify the critical risk factors and indicate the potential level of exposure. These factors are what determine the implementation of evaluation mechanism to controls, and, therefore, must determine its behavior over time to determine whether the level of risk exposure has increased or decreased [3, 11, and 12]. Determining the effectiveness of controls is a fundamental practice applied to assess risk. The result obtained by the risk analysis identifies the controls to be implemented. The risk classification obtained by the analysis will define the nature of the measurement mechanisms employed to attempt to measure the effectiveness of controls. The key to the metrics definition is the correct definition of the critical attributes of the control to measure the risk exposure of the company. The AI techniques play key role in risk management processes. The process of risk management consists of risk identification, risk assessment, and risk control. The first phase of risk management is risk identification with respect to system vulnerabilities. Risk identification is the process of determining risks that could impact the confidentiality, integrity, and availability of the information system. Based on Garvey (2008) analytical methods for risk management are illustrated in Figure 5.3.

The second step of risk management is risk assessment. Risk assessment is a key component of a holistic, organizationwide risk management process as defined in *NIST Special Publication 800-39, Managing Information Security Risk: Organization, Mission, and Information System View*. Based on NIST 800-39 document the risk assessment is illustrated in Figure 5.4.

The third step of risk management is risk control or risk treatment. The notion of this step is to develop a plan that identifies the countermeasures necessary to reduce, retain, avoid, or transfer identified risks.

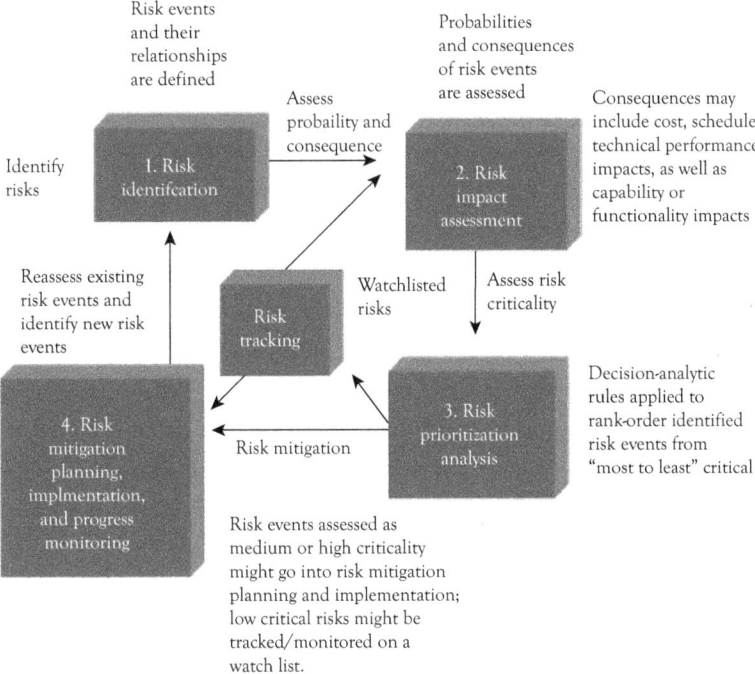

Figure 5.3 Fundamental steps in risk management

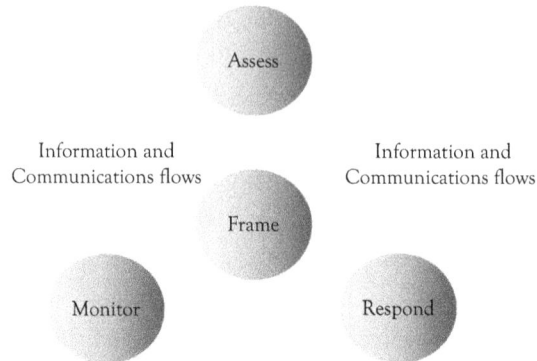

Information and   Information and
Communications flows   Communications flows

Figure 5.4 Risk assessment within risk management process

Organizations confront an uphill challenge when it comes to identification of threats, since the attack mechanism is changed from network
and endpoint to cloud services, application, and mobile devices (e.g.,
tablets, mobile phones, smart watches, and Bluetooth devices). The business model has changed from traditional business model to e-commerce,
m-commerce, and Internet of Things (IoT). As the next 50 billion IoT
devices come online by 2020, the organizations will face some apprehen-
sion challenges, such as securing the security of their devices. Also there
are challenges of the of big data to the organization which changing the
way businesses compete, and operate. Security big data is a major concern
within organization. Based on recent research which it indicates that, it
takes most of organization on average 146 days to identify the attack,
and fix the critical vulnerabilities (https://info.whitehatsec.com/rs/675-
YBI-674/images/WH-2016-Stats-Report-FINAL.pdf). This report obviously represents that we need to reconsider or reassess the existing approach
to cybersecurity. With the complexity and amount of cyber-attacks, and
also the speed of processes and the amount of data to be analyzed to
defending the organization information security systems cannot be handled by human or human intervention is simply not sufficient for timely
attack analysis, and appropriate response to the attacks. For that reason
we need a more sophisticated information security system that requires
to be flexible, adaptable, and robust (Selma 2015) and able to detect a
wide variety of threats and make intelligent real-time decisions. This is
why we need innovative methodologies such as applied AI that provide

flexibility, and machine learning capability to software, which will help human to defending cyber threats/attacks. There are tremendous benefits for cybersecurity professionals to invest AI and cognitive techniques. For example routine tasks such as analyzing large volumes of security event logs can be automated by using machine learning to increase accuracy. As systems become more effective at identifying and recognizing malware and unauthorized access, cybersecurity systems can become "self-healing" by updating controls and patching systems in real time, and as a direct result of machine learning and understanding how hackers exploit new approaches. AI methodologies can help in developing a better threat detection algorithm to secure the information security systems (Anwar). Threat detection is definitely a main focus of today's AI and machine learning technology. As we illustrated in Figure 5.5 the machine learning should be part of detecting the threat and identifying organization information systems vulnerability, and assess the risks with respect to them. Based on Selma (2015) some of the scholars such as Chaudhary et al. (2014) developed an anomaly-based fuzzy intrusion detection system to detect the packet dropping attacks in mobile ad hoc networks; Benaicha et al. (2014) presented a network intrusion detection model based on genetic algorithm, and also Padmadas et al. (2014) developed a layered genetic algorithm-based intrusion detection system for monitoring activities. There are companies using AI in cybersecurity. For example, based on CBINSIGHTS report Cylance applies the AI algorithms to predict, identify, and stop malware and mitigate damages from zero-day attacks.

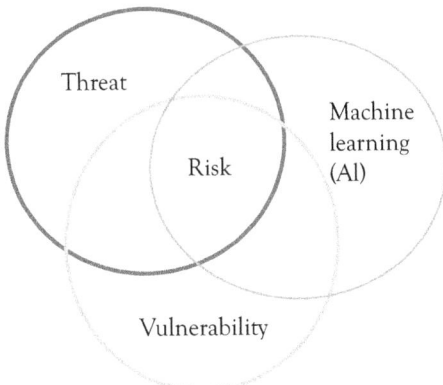

Figure 5.5 Machine learning in threat, vulnerability, and risk

Tantium, a real-time endpoint management solution that provides instant visibility into networked devices through natural language processing, allows enterprises to collect data and update machines across networks. LogRhythm offers threat intelligence and analytics, for organizations to rapidly detect, respond to, and neutralize threats, in addition to compliance automation and assurance, and enhanced IT intelligence. Darktrace pairs behavioral analytics with advanced mathematics to automatically detect abnormal behavior in organizations. RiskSense uses a contextualization engine and human-interactive machine learning technology to drive risk-based analytics and prioritize remediation actions based on business criticality. Sift Science provides real-time machine learning fraud prevention solutions for online businesses. Avata Intelligence delivers descriptive, diagnostic, predictive, and prescriptive analytics to understand and respond to security threats. E8 Security provides intelligence and analytics software alongside a big data platform for long-term data retention and retrospective analysis. Finjan's online security innovation cultivates proprietary technology that is focused on proactively detecting threats by identifying patterns and behavior of online viruses and other malicious code, rather than relying solely on lists of existing or known coded threats. F-Secure's endpoint products prevent all examples of the threat. F-Secure's vulnerability management product flags the used vulnerabilities within the system for remediation. Finally, the F-Secure-managed incident response service detects the attack and enables immediate response to the threat.

The second strategy must be to develop a holistic approach to securing, processes, and people. Processes (policy, standard, and procedures) and people are the imperative elements of an effective quality information security program by applying the AI techniques to secure information in enterprise (Figure 5.6). The mantra of a good cybersecurity is not only about technology, but it is also about people and processes. *A holistic approach to information security means that security is integrated with every part of the development life cycle (hardware, software), creating a defense in depth against vulnerabilities. This kind of approach should support the people through security training, culture of security within organization, the process through policies, standards, procedure, measurement, and metrics, and finally the technology through security assessment and support tools by embedding*

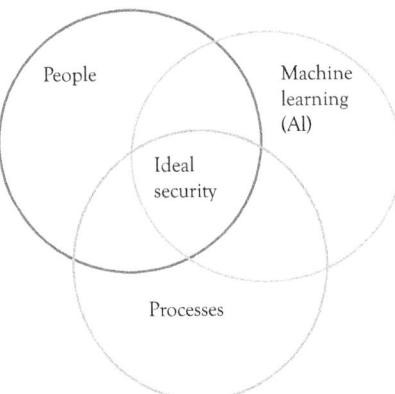

Figure 5.6 Machine learning, people, processes, and ideal security

AI. There are companies using AI in cybersecurity. For example, based on Venture radar report Exabeam offers user behavior analytics that leverages existing log data to quickly detect advanced attacks, prioritize incidents, and guide effective responses. Status Today protects companies from insider threats and data breaches using a patent-pending AI that understands human behavior. Using machine learning techniques and organizational human behavior it detects possible malicious behavior, no matter how big or small. The system doesn't intercept data or intrude in the network, which might decrease the performance, but instead uses a passive monitoring approach that sits behind the scene. Harvest aims to replicate the processes of top security researchers: searching for changes in behavior of users, key business systems, and applications caused by targeted cyber-attacks. Harvest has applied AI-based algorithms to learn the business value of critical documents across an organization, and offer what it describes as an industry-first ability to detect and stop data breaches from targeted attacks and insider threats before data is stolen. Fortscale's user and entity behavior analytics (UEBA) solution combines expertise from the Israeli Defense Force's elite security unit, big data analytics, and advanced machine learning to deliver what the company describes as the holy grail of enterprise security: The ability to rapidly detect and eliminate insider threats. From rogue employees to hackers with stolen credentials, Fortscale is designed to automatically and dynamically identify anomalous behaviors and prioritize the highest-risk activities within any application, anywhere in the enterprise network. JASK says that the tsunami of logs, SIEM (Security Information and Event Management) events, and other indicators that security analysts face every day produces a never-ending flood of unknowns, which forces these analysts to spend their valuable time sorting through indicators in the endless hunt for real threats. JASK is aiming to solve this problem by developing a new AI-based approach that can highlight the real actual attacks.

Conclusion

In recent years AI is regarded as one of the most expressing assurance developments in the information security and cybersecurity framework. In the presence of an environment of fast growing advanced attacks it is impossible to defend the organization systems without applying AI to cybersecurity. For that reason, researchers and practitioners cultivated and developed new AI techniques to enhance the cybersecurity. Obviously the new developments in knowledge-based understanding, demonstration, and dealing furthermore in machine learning can greatly increase the cybersecurity defense mechanism. These systems are more flexible, robust, and adaptable, also in following a manner helping to improve security performance, and better defend systems from sophisticated cyber threats. At the present time machine learning techniques are the most powerful tool to be applied to the cybersecurity. Despite the promising role of AI in cybersecurity framework, a holistic perspective on the cyber environment of organization is required. The mantra of a good cybersecurity is not only about technology, but it is also about people and processes. In the end, it is still human factor that matters not only the technology. It's important to understand that AI is not the answer to all our cybersecurity challenges. Like other technologies, there are pros and cons about that technology. AI and machine learning can make sense of patterns across many sets of quality, and accurate data, to build the model for machine learning purposes; however, lack of collecting accurate data affects the machine learning process. Organizations and business executive's leaders are advised to familiarize themselves with the cutting edge of AI techniques and security research to support their business operation.

References

Allen, G., and T. Chan. 2017. *Artificial Intelligence and National Security. Report.* Boston, MA: Harvard Kennedy School, Harvard University.

Anwar, A., and S.I. Hassan. 2017. "Applying Artificial Intelligence Techniques to Prevent Cyber Assaults." *International Journal of Computational Intelligence Research* 13, no. 5, pp. 883–89.

Chen, H., and F.-Y. Wang. 2005. "Guest Editors' Introduction: Artificial Intelligence for Homeland Security." *IEEE Intelligent Systems* 20, no. 5, pp. 12–16.

Chui, M. 2017. "Artificial Intelligence the Next Digital Frontier?" *McKinsey and Company Global Institute,* https://.mckinsey.com/global-themes/artificial-intelligence (accessed August 21, 2017).

Dasgupta, D. 2006. "Computational Intelligence in Cyber Security." In *Computational Intelligence for Homeland Security and Personal Safety, Proceedings of the 2006 IEEE International Conference on,* pp. 2–3.

Garvey, P.R. 2008. *Analytical Methods for Risk Management: A Systems Engineering Perspective.* Bedford, MA: Taylor & Francis Group, CRC Press.

Greengard, S. 2016. "Cybersecurity Gets Smart." *Communications of the ACM* 59, no. 5, pp. 29–31.

Hager, G.D., R. Bryant, E. Horvitz, M. Mataric, and V. Honavar. 2017. "Advances in Artificial Intelligence Require Progress Across all of Computer Science." https://arxiv.org/abs/1707.04352 (accessed August 19, 2017).

Kasprick, R., J. Hoffman, J. Straub, and E. Kim. 2016. "Cyber Security Artificial Intelligence Expert System." https://works.bepress.com/jeremy_straub/314/download/ (accessed July 7, 2017).

Landwehr, C.E. 2008. "Cybersecurity and Artificial Intelligence: From Fixing the Plumbing to smart water." *IEEE security & Privacy* 6, no. 5, pp. 3–4.

Madhok, E., A. Gupta, and N. Grover. 2016. "Artificial Intelligence Impact on Cyber Security." *IITM Journal of Management and IT* 7, no. 1, pp. 100–107.

Markov, Z., I. Russell, and B. Eberle. 2016. "Report on the 29th International Florida Artificial Intelligence Research Society Conference (FLAIRS-29)." *AI Magazine* 37, no. 4, pp. 81–83.

Merat, S., and W. Almuhtadi. 2015. "Artificial Intelligence Application for Improving Cyber-security Acquirement." In *Electrical and Computer Engineering (CCECE), 2015 IEEE 28th Canadian Conference on,* pp. 1445–50.

Mittu, R., and W. Lawless. 2015. "Human Factors in Cybersecurity and the Role for AI." In *Foundations of Autonomy and Its (Cyber) Threats: From Individual to Interdependence, AAAI Spring Symposium Series.*

Morel, B. 2011. "Artificial Intelligence and the Future of Cybersecurity." In *Proceedings of the 4th ACM Workshop on Security and Artificial Intelligence,* pp. 93–98.

National Institute of Standard Technology, NIST 800-39. 2011. "Managing Information Security Risk: Organization, Mission, and Information System View." https://csrc.nist.gov/publications/detail/sp/800-39/final (accessed August 10, 2017).

Patil, P. 2016. "Artificial Intelligence in Cyber Security." *International Journal of Research in Computer Applications & Robotics* 4, no. 5, pp. 1–5.

Pfeffer, A., B. Ruttenberg, L. Kellogg, M. Howard, C. Call, A. O'Connor, G. Takata, and et al. 2017. "Artificial Intelligence Based Malware Analysis" https://pdfs.semanticscholar.org/8e58/db5def7e10e7e442236df7c4ec01da024e1f.pdf (accessed August 19, 2017).

Rehman, A. and T. Saba. 2014. "Evaluation of Artificial Intelligent Techniques to Secure Information in Enterprises." *Artificial Intelligent Review Journal* 42, no. 4, pp. 1029–44.

Research Artificial Intelligent. 2016. "Cybersecurity's Next Step: Artificial Intelligence Is Helping Predict, Prevent, and Defeat Attacks." https://.cbinsights.com/blog/cybersecurity-artificial-intelligence/ (accessed September 10, 2017).

Russell, S., D. Dewey, and M. Tegmark. 2015. "Research Priorities for Robust and Beneficial Artificial Intelligence." *AI Magazine* 36, no. 4, pp. 105–14.

Selma, D., H. Çakır, and M. Aydın. 2015. "Applications of Artificial Intelligence Techniques to Combating Cyber Crimes: A Review." *International Journal of Artificial Intelligence & Applications (IJAIA)* 6, no. 1, pp. 20–24.

Tyugu, E. 2011. "Artificial Intelligence in Cyber Defense." In *Cyber Conflict (ICCC), 2011 IEEE 3rd International Conference on,* pp. 1–11.

Thomas, A. 2016. "10 Hot Startups Using Artificial Intelligence in cyber security." http://blog.ventureradar.com/2016/03/11/10-hot-startups-using-artificial-intelligence-in-cyber-security/ (accessed September 7, 2017).

Wirkuttis, N., and H. Klein. 2017. "Artificial Intelligence in Cybersecurity." *Cyber Intelligence, and Security Journal* 1, no. 1, pp. 21–3.

CHAPTER 6

Artificial Intelligence and Innovation Management: Improving an Innovation Portfolio Through Machine Learning

Carlos Vasquez

Introduction

Innovation is a central issue in contemporary organizations (Dodgson, Gann, and Phillips 2013b; Fagerberg and Verspagen 2009; Salter and Alexi 2013). When managed effectively, innovation can improve both the top and bottom lines of businesses worldwide (Dodgson, Gann, and Salter 2008; Tzeng 2009). However, ineffective management of innovation may lead to an organization becoming uncompetitive or reliant on technologies that, once successful, are now obsolete (Dodgson, Gann, and Phillips 2013a; Christensen 2013; Freeman and Soete 1997). Technology can facilitate effective innovation management; frameworks are useful in guiding interaction with, and use of, technologies. One such technology, which is changing the way businesses are conducted, is artificial intelligence (AI), in particular machine learning (Domingos 2015; Michalski, Carbonell, and Mitchell 2013; Kolbjornsrud, Amico, and Thomas 2016).

This chapter explores how machine learning technologies can better enable the management of innovation. In particular, it outlines how activities related to data mining, predictive analytics, statistical modeling, and administrative tasks are better performed by machines (Bose and

Mahapatra 2001; Kolbjornsrud, Amico, and Thomas 2016). It also discusses how making sense of the output of those activities, in the context of an ambiguous and nuanced business environment, is better achieved by people. It is argued that innovation managers who harness the power of machine learning technologies will be able to streamline, accelerate, and bring more effective innovations into the markets in which they operate.

Preliminary Definitions

First, it is important to define innovation management and machine learning in the context of this chapter. The definition of innovation management used in this chapter is simple: it is the processes and activities that support innovation (Dodgson, Gann, and Phillips 2013b). The definition of machine learning is less straightforward, however. Machine learning is a subset of AI (Domingos 2015), which is a broader concept, encompassing the study, design, building, and analysis of computational models of action, perception, and cognition (Honavar 2006, p. 3; Langton 1997; Minsky 1974). Machine learning then is the processes that computational systems manifest to accurately recognize patterns, discover knowledge, manage and mine data, and perform predictive analytics (Domingos 2015; Michalski, Carbonell, and Mitchell 2013).

Managing and Balancing Innovation

The nature of innovation is evolving, presenting a range of challenges in its management (Salter and Alexi 2013). The challenges of innovation management are not one-dimensional: from a managerial perspective, they include the effective organization of diverse resources, actions, choices, procedures, and practices. The management of innovation literature explores how an organization can integrate its multiple innovation processes into one comprehensive innovative approach to deploy new products and services (Sundbo 1997; Trott 2008; Dodgson, Gann, and Phillips 2013b, p. 20). Other studies in the literature discuss how organizations manage their intellectual property (Malerba and Adams 2013), how to manage the process of mergers and acquisitions that may increase a company's innovation capabilities (Ahuja and Novelli 2013), and external collaboration between companies and external entities to bring innovations to the market (Chesbrough, Vanhaverbeke, and West 2006; McKelvey 2013). This includes understanding the role of users (Franke 2013) and consumers (Osaki and Dodgson 2013) so that companies know how an innovation is used and consumed.

In the midst of these challenges, particularly relevant is the question: how should a company balance its innovation portfolio, that is, how can it better manage the radical versus incremental innovation output of a company (Dodgson, Gann, and Phillips 2013b)?

Radical innovation refers to the level of market disruption from an innovation, which is evaluated through its capacity to create new value in a given market (Christensen, Raynor, and McDonald 2015) and even through its capacity to create new categories of products and services. Incremental innovation focuses on improving internal processes, and combining and recombining internal assets and capabilities to drive overall innovation output (Tzeng 2009). This is considered a more subtle and also more common approach to innovation.

These two approaches contrast fundamentally in their impact. In attempting to find a balance between radical and incremental innovations, internal innovation capabilities, insights from market knowledge, and the evaluation of risks associated with each type of innovation are used and applied differently (Dodgson, Gann, and Phillips 2013b; Stringer 2000).

How to balance and manage an innovation portfolio is relatively unknown. This is partly because there is limited information about what a company believes a balanced innovation portfolio should be and look like and also about the ways in which individuals try to manage and achieve balance. While people are trained in structured and rational thinking in which facts drive most of the decision-making process within an organization (Locke 2005; Simon 1979), in practice decisions are often made without a full understanding of all the factors and/or full access to all information available (Gilovich, Griffin, and Kahneman 2002; Jensen et al. 2007).

Successful innovation companies clearly articulate their innovation ambition through managing their total innovation portfolio rather than specific projects (Nagji and Tuff 2012). However, many organizations lack effective management tools for managing their innovation portfolio.

In the most successful organizations, internal frameworks and capabilities are implemented to provide fast, clear, comparative, and automated analysis of the success of past innovations. In doing so, these organizations aim to provide an accurate forecast of the performance of future endeavors. For example, successful innovation companies know how to diffuse their innovations and understand when to undertake radical innovation, depending on the level of encroachment into the market (Schmidt and Druehl 2008). However, there is little evidence as to how these companies document, track, and create knowledge from their innovation diffusion. Further, successful innovation may also be underpinned by advances in technology and a careful evolution in which the level of disruption the innovation creates in a given industry is more gradual or nuanced (Norman and Verganti 2014). However, these companies may not be able to explain how this innovation evolution works in practice, in terms of the connections these different levels of disruption have with other industries, or how consumer preferences have evolved as a result.

Against this background of uncertainty experienced by companies when innovating, and to effectively manage their innovation portfolio, the provision of fast, accurate, and predictive analytics is paramount to assist in tracking past innovation efforts and forecasting the success of new ones. Such analytical power, when harnessed appropriately, can provide a comprehensive view of the impact an innovation brings into the market. Hence, knowing whether, when, what, and how an innovation is incremental or radical is useful for effective decision making.

Better Solutions—Improving an Innovation Portfolio by Learning From It

The automation of administrative tasks behind innovation, the consolidation of diverse and vast inputs from the market, and the contextualization of these with the financial and sales performance of new products and services are critical tasks for companies seeking to manage innovation effectively. Through automation and systems that learn from large datasets, innovation managers will be better equipped with more complete information about the performance, profile, and diffusion of their different innovation projects.

In this regard, there is much to embrace, explore, and exploit in the capabilities of machine learning. Data mining is a powerful process that can transform large datasets into usable knowledge (Bose and Mahapatra 2001). The financial services industry is exploring the prospect of using machine learning to profile credit scorings (Kruppa et al. 2013) and smart web-browsers exploit machine learning techniques to better enable the suggestion of targeted and retargeted advertisements based on an internaut's search behavior. Large online retailers have turned to predictive analytics to facilitate marketing specific, tailored products to a returning customer, with the aim of increasing their conversion rate while visiting an online store.

The benefits of machine learning for innovative businesses are manifold. Machine learning can streamline and provide informed solutions to managers. Innovation managers who embrace, explore, and exploit machine learning techniques will be better placed to map market expectations of their different innovation projects by gaining knowledge of how these projects operate, that is, broader understanding of potential and past customer behavior according to the characteristics of a product or a service (Tkáč and Verner 2016, p. 792). Effective innovation managers understand that machine learning algorithms can transform large amounts of data into valuable information and relevant knowledge; correctly harnessing this process provides a competitive advantage.

Effectively managing an innovation portfolio requires full understanding of which machine learning techniques can provide a company with better data management and mining capabilities. This also means understanding that a company that has robust data management and data mining frameworks can also have a robust predictive analytics output (Ali and Arıtürk 2014).

In the context of large datasets, the more data companies have at their disposal for analysis, the more they can learn. However, they also face the challenge of how to automate the analytics behind the data. Those companies that excel at transforming their current frameworks and capabilities to accomplish this will have a technological advantage over their competitors (Domingos 2015). For example, within the financial services industry, companies can use these techniques to better equip their managers in making more accurate and fact-based decisions related to future investments according to market trends (Kolbjornsrud, Amico, and Thomas 2016).

Businesses that understand how to integrate the power of machine learning are better able to exploit their benefits. For instance, online retailers are better placed to understand how browsing patterns provide rich datasets to personalize consumers' shopping experience and segment their catalogs accordingly (Baluja 2006; Mobasher 2007).

Innovation Manager—Machine Interaction for Improved Management

Companies that have successfully provided a framework and the internal capabilities for computational systems to learn from the dynamics of an innovation portfolio will realize that innovation managers are no longer *users* of information but rather *interactors* with the machines providing it (Suchman 1990). This means that the management of innovation should clearly state the role that humans and machines have in the interaction.

In the context of human-machine interaction, having a clear intention, allowing the machine to make an accurate selection of the action resulting from such intention, and executing the action make human evaluation of the results of such execution possible (Norman 1984). The successful interaction of innovation managers with machines implies a clear characterization of what the manager wants the system to provide, in other words, the innovation manager can identify the future action intended, and the machine recognizes the intention and complies with an action accordingly (Tahboub 2006, p. 36). For example, an innovation manager wants to understand the financial impact of past innovation considering a specific time frame and the resultant increase in net revenue. The machine in turn will comply with this request, the intention of which is to understand the performance and financial impact of the company's innovation portfolio.

Certainly, this type of request can be done—and still is mostly done—by people. However, in the face of larger and larger datasets becoming available, having machines perform these tasks means companies will have faster and more accurate answers (Kolbjornsrud, Amico, and Thomas 2016; Domingos 2015; Bose and Mahapatra 2001). The sheer speed in the provision of information and knowledge means that the decision-making process itself is faster, with the potential to increase a company's market competitiveness.

Machines are better at data management, mining, and predictive analytics if the right technological capabilities are put in place. In terms of managing an innovation portfolio, the machines will own the calculation of *probabilities* of success of a company's innovative endeavor but the *possibilities* will still belong to humans.

Conclusion

This chapter discusses how effective management of innovation can improve the overall performance of organization. To be effective, however, companies must embrace technological advances, such as machine learning, to improve the way in which innovation is managed. In particular, this chapter focused on the potential of machine learning techniques to improve the overall management of a company's innovation portfolio by providing faster, better, and more accurate information obtained from large datasets.

Exploring the possibilities of machine learning in the context of innovation management is an ongoing and evolving endeavor, in part because machine learning techniques are in a nascent stage. Despite this, some industries are already exploiting the capabilities that these techniques provide.

At the moment, these technologies allow us to command the lights to be turned on, to find out the weather forecast for today, or to dial a colleague with a simple voice command. Our command can be acted upon almost instantaneously. Soon, these same technologies will allow innovation managers to ask for—and almost instantaneously receive—the financial contribution made by a set of new products or services in the company's profit and loss statement, how the consumer received an innovation initiative, and even what is the probability of success of an innovation project based on previous innovation efforts and market input. There is much potential to be exploited in machine learning capabilities for innovation managers.

But always, in the human–machine interaction, there is a role for humans. In the age of larger and larger datasets, innovation managers embracing machine learning techniques must also understand that making sense of complex information is still a human endeavor.

References

Ahuja, G., and E. Novelli. 2013. "Mergers and Acquisitions and Innovation." In *The Oxford Handbook of Innovation Management*, eds. M. Dodgson, D.M. Gann, and N. Phillips, 430–45. Oxford, UK: Oxford University Press.

Ali, Ö.G., and U. Arıtürk. 2014. "Dynamic Churn Prediction Framework with More Effective Use of Rare Event Data: The Case of Private Banking." *Expert Systems with Applications* 41, no. 17, pp. 7889–903.

Baluja, S. 2006. "Browsing on Small Screens: Recasting Web-Page Segmentation into an Efficient Machine Learning Framework." In *Proceedings of the 15th International Conference on World Wide Web*, 33–42. ACM. http://dl.acm.org/citation.cfm?id=1135788

Bose, I., and K.R. Mahapatra. 2001. "Business Data Mining—a Machine Learning Perspective." *Information & Management* 39, no. 3, pp. 211–25.

Chesbrough, H., W. Vanhaverbeke, and J. West. 2006. *Open Innovation: Researching a New Paradigm*. Oxford: Oxford University Press on Demand.

Christensen, C. 2013. *The Innovator's Dilemma: When New Technologies Cause Great Firms to Fail*. Boston, USA: Harvard Business Review Press.

Christensen, C., M. Raynor, and R. McDonald. 2015. "Disruptive Innovation." *Harvard Business Review* 93, no. 12, pp. 44–53.

Dodgson, M., M.D. Gann, and N. Phillips. 2013a. "Organizational Learning and the Technology of Foolishness: The Case of Virtual Worlds at IBM." *Organization Science* 24, no. 5, pp. 1358–76.

Dodgson, M., M.D. Gann, and N. Phillips. 2013b. "Perspectives on Innovation Management." In *The Oxford Handbook of Innovation Management*, eds. M. Dodgson, D.M. Gann, and N. Phillips, 3–26. Oxford, UK: Oxford University Press.

Dodgson, M., M.D. Gann, and A. Salter. 2008. *The Management of Technological Innovation: Strategy and Practice*. Oxford: Oxford University Press on Demand.

Domingos, P. 2015. *The Master Algorithm: How the Quest for the Ultimate Learning Machine Will Remake Our World*. New York, NY: Basic Books.

Fagerberg, J., and B. Verspagen. 2009. "Innovation Studies—The Emerging Structure of a New Scientific Field." *Research Policy* 38, no. 2, 218–33. doi:10.1016/j.respol.2008.12.006

Franke, N. 2013. "User-Driven Innovation." In *The Oxford Handbook of Innovation Management*, eds. M. Dodgson, D.M. Gann, and N. Phillips, 69–83. Oxford, UK: Oxford University Press.

Freeman, C., and L. Soete. 1997. *The Economics of Industrial Innovation*. Abingdon, UK: Routledge.

Gilovich, T., D. Griffin, and D. Kahneman. 2002. *Heuristics and Biases: The Psychology of Intuitive Judgment*. Cambridge, UK: Cambridge University Press.

Honavar, V. 2006. "Artificial Intelligence: An Overview." http://web.cs.iastate.edu/~cs572/handout1.pdf

Jensen, M.B., B. Johnson, E. Lorenz, and B.Å. Lundvall. 2007. "Forms of Knowledge and Modes of Innovation." *Research Policy* 36, no. 5, 680–93. doi:10.1016/j.respol.2007.01.006

Kolbjornsrud, V., R. Amico, and J.R. Thomas. 2016. "How Artificial Intelligence Will Redefine Management." *Harvard Business Review*.

Kruppa, J., A. Schwarz, G. Arminger, and A. Ziegler. 2013. "Consumer Credit Risk: Individual Probability Estimates Using Machine Learning." *Expert Systems with Applications* 40, no. 13, pp. 5125–31.

Langton, C.G. 1997. *Artificial Life: An Overview*. Cambridge, USA: Mit Press.

Locke, E.A. 2005. "Why Emotional Intelligence Is an Invalid Concept." *Journal of Organizational Behavior* 26, no. 4, pp. 425–31.

Malerba, F., and P. Adams. 2013. "Sectorial Systems of Innovation." In *The Oxford Handbook of Innovation Management*, eds. M. Dodgson, D.M. Gann, and N. Phillips, 163–83. Oxford, UK: Oxford University Press.

McKelvey, M. 2013. "Science, Technology and Business Innovation." In *The Oxford Handbook of Innovation Management*, eds. M. Dodgson, D.M. Gann, and N. Phillips, 69–82. Oxford, UK: Oxford University Press.

Michalski, R.S., J.G. Carbonell, and T.M. Mitchell. 2013. *Machine Learning: An Artificial Intelligence Approach*. California, U.S.: Springer Science & Business Media.

Minsky, M. 1974. *A Framework for Representing Knowledge*. Memo No. 306. Artificial Intelligence. Boston, Mass: Massachusetts Institute of Technology. http://18.7.29.232/handle/1721.1/6089

Mobasher, B. 2007. "Data Mining for Web Personalization." In *The Adaptive Web*, 90–135. Springer. http://link.springer.com/chapter/10.1007/978-3-540-72079-9_3

Nagji, B., and G. Tuff. 2012. "Managing Your Innovation Portfolio." *Harvard Business Review*, Spotlight, 1 (May), pp. 1–9.

Norman, D.A. 1984. "Stages and Levels in Human-Machine Interaction." *International Journal of Man-Machine Studies* 21, no. 4, pp. 365–75.

Norman, D.A., and R. Verganti. 2014. "Incremental and Radical Innovation: Design Research vs. Technology and Meaning Change." *Design Issues* 30, no. 1, pp. 78–96.

Osaki, R., and M. Dodgson. 2013. "Consumption of Innovation." In *The Oxford Handbook of Innovation Management*, eds. M. Dodgson, D.M. Gann, and N. Phillips, 248–71. Oxford, UK: Oxford University Press.

Salter, A., and O. Alexi. 2013. "The Nature of Innovation." In *The Oxford Handbook of Innovation Management*, eds. M. Dodgson, D.M. Gann, and N. Phillips, 26–50. Oxford, UK: Oxford University Press.

Schmidt, G.M., and T.C. Druehl. 2008. "When Is a Disruptive Innovation Disruptive?" *Journal of Product Innovation Management* 25, no. 4, pp. 347–69.

Simon, H.A. 1979. "Rational Decision Making in Business Organizations." *The American Economic Review* 69, no. 4, pp. 493–513.

Stringer, R. 2000. "How to Manage Radical Innovation." *California Management Review* 42, no. 4, pp. 70–88.

Suchman, L.A. 1990. "What Is Human-Machine Interaction." *Cognition, Computing, and Cooperation*, pp. 25–55.

Sundbo, J. 1997. "Management of Innovation in Services." *Service Industries Journal* 17, no. 3, pp. 432–55.

Tahboub, K.A. 2006. "Intelligent Human-Machine Interaction Based on Dynamic Bayesian Networks Probabilistic Intention Recognition." *Journal of Intelligent & Robotic Systems* 45, no. 1, pp. 31–52.

Tkáč, M., and R. Verner. 2016. "Artificial Neural Networks in Business: Two Decades of Research." *Applied Soft Computing* 38, pp. 788–804.

Trott, P. 2008. *Innovation Management and New Product Development [4th Ed.]/ Chapter 12: New Product Development*. Essex: England: Prentice Hall.

Tzeng, C.-H. 2009. "A Review of Contemporary Innovation Literature: A Schumpeterian Perspective." *Innovation* 11, no. 3, 373–94. doi:10.5172/impp.11.3.373

CHAPTER 7

Permissionless Evolution of Ethics—Artificial Intelligence

Margaret A. Goralski and Krystyna Górniak-Kocikowska

When Darwin introduced the theory of evolution, a deep change occurred not only in science, but also in many unanticipated areas including Western ethical theory. Similarly, the development of computer science, along with other emerging and converging technologies, especially robotics and artificial intelligence (AI), is causing a profound change to ethical theories as well as to the critical decision-making process necessary to define the ethics and morals of killer robots, in the case of autonomous drones, missiles, and the more ubiquitous autonomous cars.

One can look at AI as the result of the convergence of two approaches to knowledge that have dominated Western civilization since ancient times; one of them focused on humans, and the other on the world. AI is the result of a growing knowledge about the world (science and technology) as well as a deeper understanding of humans—not only human biology but also human values, including the ethical values—and both areas of knowledge are necessary for creation of human-like intelligence, which AI is supposed to be. Moreover, in order to interact with humans effectively and also for commercial success, AI has to be *human-like*, at least for the near future.

However, the recent, very rapid ascendance of the importance of AI and AI-related research makes feasible a theory, which has been discussed for some time; namely, that AI could (some think it will) self-evolve and become autonomous. The authors would like to further explore the ethical consequences of such a possibility.

In the early days, computer scientists who worked on the creation of AI were not particularly interested in exploring ethical issues related to AI. They were focused mainly on the challenges posed by the attempts to approximate the way computer programs "think" to the way humans think. Their main interest was in what was possible. They questioned whether computers could be taught to think like humans.

In those days, ethical questions and concerns related to AI were voiced mainly by philosophers and sci-fi writers. Many of them worked under the assumption that anything and everything would be possible in the AI arena eventually. They were creating thought experiments on yet another assumption, namely, that AI could approximate human intelligence to the point of making the two indistinguishable. For instance, Philip K. Dick, author of the book *Do Androids Dream of Electric Sheep* on which the movie *Blade Runner* was based, wrote about androids exploiting the boundaries between human and machine. In his imagined future, androids were so sophisticated that they could look just like a human and could be programmed to believe that they were human, complete with fake childhood memories. People would wonder if their friends and loved ones were really human, but most of all they would wonder about themselves—if they were really human. Identity confusion was a recurring theme in Dick's work. Then, David Hanson created a replica of Philip K. Dick in 2005, with true-to-life artificial skin that looks real and the intelligence to be able to think, feel, build relationships with people as "he" understands one's speech. The artificial Philip K. Dick can carry on a natural conversation while his computer brain gathers information about the questioner and evolves by constructing responses and formulating facial mannerisms that mimic the questioner (Goralski and Gorniak-Kocikowska 2014).

For quite a while, AI-related ethical issues were treated by philosophers and science fiction writers as being similar to or sometimes even identical with human-related ethical problems. Not only was AI dealt with from an *anthropocentric* point of view, it was also *anthropomorphic.* It is only recently that discussion of AI is moving past the confines of human brains and therefore beyond the domain of *human* thought.

Recently, AI reached the point of commercial viability and its development and commercial applications accelerated greatly. The presence of AI will soon be ubiquitous in a wide range of areas where it will interact with humans or otherwise have an impact on human lives. This causes understandable concern voiced by some top scientists and AI experts such as Stephen Hawking and Elon Musk (Cuthbertson 2017; Shead 2017). Instilling ethics and morals into AI has become of critical importance.

Human ethics pertains to human actions and interactions being judged as moral or immoral, ethical or unethical. The process is difficult and often confusing for many reasons, one of them being that there are—in the Western civilization alone—several different, often competing, ethical theories. Another difficulty is caused by the fact that there is no clear line separating these two terms, ethics and morals. They are frequently used as synonyms, which can significantly amplify the already difficult and often confusing issues under discussion. However, the majority of philosophers think of ethics as a theory of morality (moral theory) in which case morality is seen as the practical application—affirmative or negative—of one's ethical beliefs and judgments. In this chapter, we will follow this distinction.

In general, there are two fundamental ethical questions: (1). How can one know for certain what is the right (good) thing to do? (2). How can one make other people, possibly all people, take the right (good) action? Obviously, these are questions not only of great importance but of great complexity and difficulty as well. Western philosophers (the authors purposefully omit non-Western traditions due to the space restraints for this essay) have been discussing these issues at least since the age of Socrates and Plato. Ethics also constitutes a huge component of most religious systems worldwide. Yet in "real life" there is still no agreement how to answer the two questions mentioned above.

Ethics, as a theory, is meant usually to apply to the entire humankind (to be universal). However, it is sometimes directed purposefully to just one particular group of people. Such is the case with professional ethics. The need for the establishment of professional ethics is closely related to the fact that many activities particular to a profession and not related to other areas of human life are subject to ethical/moral judgment. With the development of the modern concept of "profession" numerous professional ethics were established, among them business ethics (Moriarty 2016) and computer ethics (ICT ethics), and now AI ethics.

Darwin's theory generated ideas Darwin himself most likely did not anticipate such as, among others, the creation of environmental ethics and animal ethics, which are different from the earlier ethical *concerns* regarding animals, where animal well-being was basically intended to serve the purpose of making *humans* into better beings (in an ethical sense). Environmental and animal ethics today are ethical theories in which *anthropocentrism* is significantly weakened. There seems to be a progressing emancipation of these new branches of ethics from the controlling power of a human-centered approach and a shift toward a more co-existential and possibly a dialogical one. That is probably one of the chief reasons why the *anthropomorphic* approach to the nonhuman environment remains quite strong.

Just as in the case of Darwin's theory of evolution, with its unforeseen consequences for ethics, so today, too, the development of AI and its commercial applications change ethics, opening new fields of investigation and new vistas in the old ones.

The AI revolution leads to even greater challenges than those caused by Darwin's theory. This includes ethics. Assuming AI's ability to self-evolve and to become autonomous, one should also accept the possibility of AI creating its own value system, ethical values being of greatest interest here. Therefore, a differentiation should be made between *AI ethics* as a branch of human professional ethics, meant for humans whose profession it is to deal with AI in a variety of ways, and the *ethics of AI* as ethics created by AI for itself (at this point, let's treat it as an AI equivalent of universal human ethics). The problem of AI-related ethics (both AI ethics and the ethics of AI) is a tremendously important, but also tremendously complex, issue for a variety of reasons but mainly because it enters truly uncharted territories.

In 2014, researchers were exploring how they might create robots endowed with their own sense of morality.

A group of researchers from Tufts University, Brown University, and Rensselaer Polytechnic Institute were collaborating with the U.S. Navy in a multi-year effort to explore how they might create robots endowed with their own sense of morality. If the researchers were successful, then they would create an artificial intelligence that was able to autonomously assess a difficult situation and then make a complex ethical decision that could override the instructions that it had been given (Borghino 2014, para. 1).

The technology advanced from this project could be used to assist soldiers in battle via medical robots, but the technology could also be turned into a sophisticated war machine.

Joseph R. Carvalko (2014) discussed how easy it is to turn a machine that was made for humanitarian purposes into a machine that could be made for war. "We trained our creation to recognize how to tell a river from a riverbank, how to tell a boat from a river, how to tell a sampan from a patrol boat, but unfortunately not how to tell a good guy, military or civilian, from a bad guy" (para. 17). He stated that it was ironic how technology that was so beneficial or neutral could more times than not degenerate into a weapon of war (One should remember though that humans too do not always know "how to tell a good guy, military or civilian, from a bad guy.").

John Markoff (2014) writes about an Air Force B-1 bomber that was launched as an experimental missile. The pilots would direct the missile, but then halfway to its destination communication would be severed with the operators and, without human oversight, the missile on its own would determine which of three ships to attack—striking a 260-foot unmanned freighter. This is the future, and to some degree already the reality, of warfare—wars guided by software. Drones that can be operated by humans remotely miles away, but more commonly wars that will be carried out by weapons that rely on AI without human intervention. Weapons are becoming smarter and nimbler—increasingly difficult for humans to control or defend against. "Britain, Israel, and Norway are already deploying missiles and drones that carry out attacks against enemy radar, tanks, and ships without direct human control" (Markoff 2014, para. 5).

Representatives from 87 nations, United Nation agencies, the International Committee of the Red Cross, and the Campaign to Stop Killer Robots met for the first multilateral meeting in May 2014 to confront the challenge of fully autonomous weapons that could select and attack targets without human control. The United Nations special rapporteur Christof Heyns asked for a moratorium on development of these kinds of weapons, but government intervention and concerns will not deter the development of advanced autonomous weapons that can kill without oversight. Military analysts argue that autonomous smart weapons reduce casualties and indiscriminate killing (Markoff 2014). "We must be vigilant to spot those instances where scientific progress serves peace and reconciliation on the one hand and war on the other, or how technology fortifies effectiveness in a national vital endeavor, but weakens our cherished values" (Carvalko 2014, p. 22).

AI already supplants human decisions in a variety of fields: medical diagnostics (IBM's famous Watson; APACHE medical systems), driverless trains in cities worldwide (Lin 2013), and Wall Street's high-speed stock trading floor. Nick Bostrom (2008), Oxford Future of Humanity Institute, states:

We will have superhuman artificial intelligence within the first third of the next century ... We can expect superintelligence to be developed once there is human-level artificial intelligence ... By a "superintelligence" we mean an intellect that is much smarter than the best human brains in practically every field, including scientific creativity, general wisdom and social skills. (para. 1 and 2)

Once AI reaches a point where it could improve itself and create other intelligent forms of AI, then these more powerful superintelligences could prevail.

Many AI and robotic ethicists argue that Asimov's "Three Laws of Robotics" are too simplistic for our contemporary world. Asimov's laws are clearly directed to the creators of AI, that is, to computer scientists. He follows the idea that the main purpose of the creation and development of AI is to make it human-like as perfectly, as possible. The new approach is that with the sophistication of computers and integration of AI into human lives, a new set of laws are required (Cuthbertson 2017). Stephen Hawking and Tesla CEO Elon Musk have created a set of 23 principles—the Asilomar AI Principles, which establish guidelines to help self-thinking machines remain safe for humans and "act in humanity's best interest" (Shead 2017). Musk believes that AI has the potential to be more damaging than nuclear weapons and Hawking believes that AI has the potential to end humanity. On the other hand, they believe that AI could slow global warming or find a cure for cancer (Shead 2017).

According to Ronald Arkin, director of the mobile robot laboratory at Georgia Institute of Technology, "The issues of morality in general are very vague … We still argue as human beings about the correct moral framework we should use … consequentialist utilitarian or Kantian deontological" (Goldhill 2016, para. 5). Philosophers, computer scientists, cosmologists, and business people are all grappling with the future ethics and morality of robots and AI because the future is now.

Once confined to the minds of science fiction writers, a car that would drive itself was a vision for the future. One did not have to think about how to instill ethics and morals into autonomous cars. While a human driver might be forgiven for swerving into traffic rather than hitting a pedestrian, would an automated car have that same leeway or should programmers and designers be held responsible for not programming in the most ethical decision? Will they be able to agree upon what kind of ethics to program into the car's computer? Will an autonomous car know and be able to choose the lesser of two evils? Lin (2013) asks, "Is it better to save an adult or child? What about saving two (or three or ten) adults versus one child?" Hawking (2017) asks similar questions. Programmers will have to think about and factor in all of these difficult decisions. They will have to foresee a myriad of scenarios and set forth guiding principles for each scenario (Lin 2013). "It matters to the issue of responsibility and ethics whether an act was premeditated (as in the case of programming a robot car) or reflexively without any deliberation (as may be the case with human drivers in sudden crashes)" (Lin 2013, para. 17). Programmers and designers will have to foresee all kinds of mundane occurrences, for example, a dog running into traffic as well as lesser scenarios, which might happen rarely but still be fatal. Lin brings up many future responsibilities of not only programmers and designers, but also of society itself and even the car, for example, should a car be loyal to its owner and value his/her life more than unknown drivers or pedestrians; would the AI of robot cars with a highly developed sense of self-identity try to protect itself from destruction in a crash; would robot cars be more or less susceptible to hacking; could other drivers be tempted to "game" an autonomous car forcing it to slow down or swerve. However, according to Grey (2014), "Autonomous cars don't have to be perfect, they just need to be better than us. Human drivers kill 40,000 people a year with cars just in the United States" (2014).

Ethics and morals are difficult to reduce into algorithms (Lin 2016), but this is the contemporary world. There are profound changes in ethical theories as well as in the critical decision-making process that is necessary to define the ethics and morals of killer robots, missiles, and—on the other end of the spectrum—robotic caregivers, doctors, and teachers, but especially in the more ubiquitous but imminent use of autonomous cars. Since 2006, when the Pentagon's research agency offered a $2 million prize to gather new ideas for the future of unmanned warfare by challenging entrepreneurs and universities to create a driverless car, until today, there have been great strides in the development of autonomous cars. With almost all car manufacturers now competing for this market, autonomous cars are a reality.

Humankind is experiencing a profound permissionless evolution of ethics as AI has gained prominence from the minds of philosophers and science fiction writers to the reality of a world where numerous writers from a variety of fields are stating that humans no longer need apply since this new evolution of AI will make them defunct (Gray 2014; Kolbert 2016). Ethics and morals have become more prominent in all walks of life since AI has become so ubiquitous.

Thus far, the consensus is that AI is purely rational and there are strong indicators that it already can surpass the rational thinking of even exceptionally smart people. Therefore, there is a possibility of AI perfecting one of the rational ethical systems created by humans (for instance, Kant's ethics or Utilitarianism) and deliver an unquestionable proof for the superiority of that ethical system over all other ethical systems created by humans, thus eliminating them. It could also be possible that AI would develop a perfectly rational ethical system different from any of those created thus far by humans simply for the reason that humans lack the capacity to do so; humans would create such a system, if they were able to. In both cases this could happen if self-evolving AI remains anthropomorphic, the way it has been first created. Also in both cases there should not be a great dissonance, if any, between humans and AI over ethics, providing that humans would accept to act on the ethical principles worked out by AI. Would they? Ever since Asimov, all the way to Hawking, the approach that "We must make sure we control AI and not it us" and that AI should be engaged "in the service of humans" (Penn 2017) has been unquestionable. Bill Gates, co-founder of Microsoft, and Hawking have warned of the dangers of AI becoming too powerful for humans to control (Ashrafian 2015). However, the authors believe that humans must think of ways for humankind to survive or even flourish even when not in control of AI and when AI won't continue to *serve* humans, which is the situation that Gates and Hawking among others worry about. Such a situation *is possible* and perhaps *inevitable*. The authors also accept the possibility, or even likelihood, of self-evolving autonomous AI evolving in a direction different from being anthropomorphic and creating for itself (and acting accordingly) a non-anthropocentric ethics that would not acknowledge human superiority. It even could be incompatible with any human ethics. That, of course, would be the most serious and important problem for humans to solve. However, due to the limitations of this chapter, this option will not be discussed, but this issue should be examined very carefully and seriously in the near future.

References

Ashrafian, H. March 26, 2015. "Intelligent Robots Must Uphold Human Rights." *Nature* 519, p. 391.

Borghino, D. May 13, 2014. "Scientists Try to Teach Robots Morality." *Tufts University.* http://newatlas.com/machine-ethics-artificial-intelligence/32036/

Bostrom, N. 1997, 1998, 2000, 2005, 2008. "How Long Before Superintelligence?" https://.nickbostrom.com/superintelligence.html

Carvalko, J.R. 2014. "Self Absorption." *Institute for Ethics and Emerging Technologies.* https://ieet.org/index.php/IEET/more/carvalko20141219 (accessed December 14, 2014).

Cuthbertson, A. 2017. "Elon Musk and Stephen Hawking Warn of Artificial Intelligence Arms Race." *Newsweek.* http://.newsweek.com/ai-asilomar-principles-artificial-intelligence-elon-musk-550525 (accessed January 13, 2017).

Goldhill, O. April 3, 2016. "Can we trust robots to make moral decisions?" *Quartz Media.* https://qz.com/653575/can-we-trust-robots-to-make-moral-decisions/ (accessed January 3, 2016).

Goralski, M., and K. Górniak-Kocikowska. 2014. "A New Frontier in Ethics Education: Robotics," paper presented at the Academy of International Business—Northeast Chapter Special Conference, Tianjin China (accessed January 11, 2014).

Gray, C.G.P. 2014. "Humans Need Not Apply." *YouTube.* https://.youtube.com/watch?v=7Pq-S557XQU (accessed August 13, 2014).

Kolbert, E. 2016. "Our Automated Future—How long will it be before you lose your job to a robot?" *The New Yorker.* http://.newyorker.com/magazine/2016/12/19/our-automated-future (accessed December 19 and 26, 2016).

Lin, P. 2016. "Why Ethics Matters for Autonomous Cars." In *Autonomous Driving*, 69–85. Berlin Heidelberg: Springer.

Lin, P. 2013. "The Ethics of Autonomous Cars." *The Atlantic.* https://.theatlantic.com/technology/archive/2013/10/the-ethics-of-autonomous-cars/280360/ (accessed October 8, 2013).

Markoff, J. "Fearing Bombs that Can Pick Whom to Kill." *The New York Times.* https://.nytimes.com/2014/11/12/science/weapons-directed-by-robots-not-humans-raise-ethical-questions.html?mcubz=1 (accessed November 11, 2014).

Moriarty, J. 2016. "Business Ethics." *Stanford Encyclopedia of Philosophy.* https://plato.stanford.edu/entries/ethics-business/ (accessed November 17, 2016).

Penn, F. 2017. "Stephen Hawking: Self-Evolving Artificial Intelligence (AI) Has a Free Will & May Destroy H." *YouTube.* https://.youtube.com/watch?v=U2yhVCTC4sg

Robin, M.H. "Death by Robot." *The New York Times Magazine*, MM16 (accessed January 11, 2015).

Shead, S. 2017. "Stephen Hawking and Elon Musk Backed 23 Principles to Ensure Humanity Benefits from AI." *Business Insider.* http://.businessinsider.com/stephen-hawking-elon-musk-backed-asimolar-ai-principles-for-artificial-intelligence-2017-2 (accessed February 1, 2017).

CHAPTER 8

The Future of Logistics and Marketing in an Artificial Intelligence-Governed World

Luis A. Soto and Sergio Biggemann

Introduction

In the quest of attracting and keeping satisfied customers, businesses rely heavily on marketing strategies and their execution puts logistics processes under significant strain. It is no news anymore that customers are becoming not only better informed thanks to the evolution of digital technology and availability of social media platforms accessible at any moment through smartphones and other means, but also their expectations of immediate response, product availability, service quality, and low price are constantly increasing. Consequently, marketers continuously figure out new strategies to increase service levels to protect their customers' base. Seeming like a vicious circle, customers elevate their expectations even more, making logistics processes growingly complex.

The good news is that, in the same form that digital technology increased customers' expectations, it has affected product life cycles and encouraged customers' consumption. It also made possible the execution of new logistics processes that prior to the introduction of new technology were unthinkable. Due to digital technologies, marketers and logistics managers are able to better understand customers' needs. Given that the level of knowledge that businesses have about customers has also increased significantly with the accessibility of information using smartphones.

Estimates on smartphones penetration indicate that 44 percent of the world population own one. As it is well known, most smartphones have a GPS incorporated, thus carrying a smartphone everywhere a person goes (like most people do) is equivalent to be broadcasting your geographical position 24/7. This allows marketers to know not only where their customers are, but in combination with other data collection instruments, such as digital means of payment, marketers also know what are they buying and when. If it were not sufficient, people's interests are also captured through information of what Internet pages they visit and the kind of product they search for. Orwell's 1984 imagination fell short compared with today's reality (Orwell 1949). However, the list of occurrences related to the advances of digital technology goes further and includes: the Internet of things (IoT), Drones, conversational interfaces, engagement platforms, machine learning, and big data to mention a few. Each one impacts the logistics capabilities of businesses and has the potential to satisfy their customers' constantly growing needs and demands.

Logistics is often perceived as the process capabilities displayed by a business to make demand meet supply and marketing. Driven by businesses strategies it creates value propositions for their target market. Being in the crossroad of marketing, logistics, and markets, a smart logistics and marketing ecosystem, it is often shaped by digital technology. See Figure 8.1 for illustration.

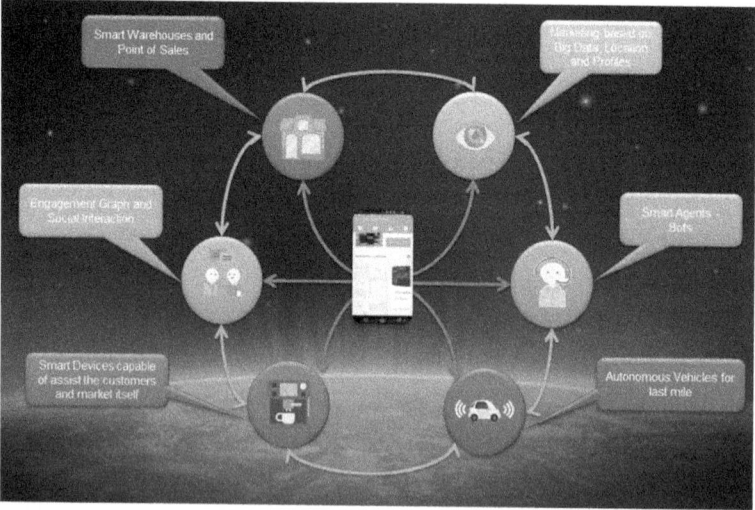

Figure 8.1 The smart logistics and marketing ecosystem

This chapter discusses how marketing and logistics have been in constant change and evolution driven by changes in digital technology. However, this model now faces an even more significant change due to the increased infusion of artificial intelligence (AI) in the system. The basis of logistics systems and its intersection with marketing is first discussed, followed by the technological occurrences and their effects in marketing logistics systems, and the infusion of AI in marketing logistics systems. The chapter concludes with viewpoints on the future of marketing logistics in an AI-governed world.

The Marketing Logistics System

The authors liberally mix logistics and supply chain management functions and refer to both only as logistics. However, it is acknowledged that sometimes there is confusion of what processes belong to what function. Context can be derived by drawing from the Council of Logistics Management definition of logistics: "the process of planning, implementing, and controlling the efficient, effective flow and storage of goods, services, and related information from point of origin to point of consumption for the purpose of conforming to customer requirements" (Wood 1998) and Lummus et al. (2001) view of supply chain management as inclusive of logistical flows, customer order management, and production process. Additionally, the marketing definition of the American Marketing Association is: "Marketing is the activity, set of institutions, and processes for creating, communicating, delivering, and exchanging offerings that have value for customers, clients, partners, and society at large" (AMA 2013). From these definitions, it could be argued that the role of logistics is to support marketing value creation endeavors, a task that is achieved in fulfilling customers' orders where the intersection between marketing and logistics is found. The processes under logistics management include inventory planning and management, procurement and supplier management, transportation, and warehouse. These all aim to maximize customer service while minimizing costs.

Marketing and logistics managers meet customers' orders and work together in planning and controlling the flows of information, goods, and payments between parties in the logistics and marketing ecosystem. With the proliferation of digital technology, all these activities led to a smarter logistics and marketing ecosystem that better satisfied customer orders. With regard to the management of product, information, and payments flows, the most onerous is the flow of products. However, the three flows are intertwined. Unless proper information of delivery requirements becomes available, logistics processes cannot be instigated. For instance, unless the products reach the correct destination, payments cannot be collected. It is through payments that the system becomes viable. The effect of digital technology in these three flows has been fundamental in the development of marketing activities over the recent time.

Digital Technology

Digital technology facilitates the flows of products by making the flows of information and payments faster and more accurate. Information is especially important to achieving high levels of customer service. Information flows start with demand, through which logistics managers plan inventory levels. The greater the accuracy in forecasting demand, the lower the inventory levels. However, the greater the marketing activity, the more difficult it has been traditionally to reduce demand forecast errors. A typical business response is to increase inventory levels. This leads to higher inventory carrying costs in order to secure high customer service levels and to reduce cost of lost sales. Therefore, the tension between cost minimization and customer service maximization is permanent. However, advances in digital technology improved information availability that has not only reduced the tension, but also allowed businesses to increase customer service while reducing inventory management costs. In the digitalization of businesses interaction, the Internet has been the main driver for improvement, but also stands as the main challenge that marketing logistics has confronted.

The most visible effect of the Internet has been the development of e-commerce. Its adoption was so spectacular that, in the early days, businesses embarked in e-commerce ventures without the adequate logistics capabilities to fulfill the orders of their newly acquired customers. In 2000, the dot.com bubble finally burst causing significant losses in several markets. However, it was also the enabler of more affordable Internet access for both customers and businesses. For the first time, businesses had access to unlimited worldwide markets, while customers could buy anything from anywhere in the world. It required some time to pass until the capabilities for physical delivery were put in place, but eventually this has become the new business reality. Unlimited markets, despite its attractiveness, create significant challenges for logistics operators. They are the party responsible for delivering the goods in the right place at the right time at a minimum cost. Their activities include: coordinating customer orders with inventory availability, either at the firms' own warehouses or at suppliers' warehouses, engaging transportation services for delivery, sharing relevant customer information, and collecting the payments on time. Efficient logistics operations could only be achieved by creating a processes capable of understanding the behavior of each actor in the system and managing its information efficiently. Traditional systems have been incapable of achieving this goal; however, digital technology has proven to be of great utility. Among the digitally enabled processes are the following: electronics means of payment, electronic data interchange (EDI), radio-frequency identification (RFID), smart devices with GPS capabilities, beacons, drones, IoT, conversational interfaces, engagement platforms, and machine learning systems. Some of the previous are purely digital technology enabled processes. Others are the first signs of AI applied to marketing logistics.

Electronics Means of Payment and Data Interchange

Processes of payments and data interchange are combined in this section because they are more or less contemporary and had produced similar effects to the supply chain, in regard to reducing errors of information and payment exchange. Both offer positive influence in time reduction and customer service levels. Data transfer errors could mean delays in placing orders as well as in receiving payments. In the past, EDI was only accessible to large organizations. Today buyers from all types of organizations including individuals can place their purchase orders by selecting items directly from sellers' databases, minimizing re-typing mistakes. Electronic exchange of both information and payments affects all processes in the supply chain, from customers to the firm and vice versa, and from the firm to their suppliers of goods, of services, and transportation. Digital technology made it possible for firms to create visibility on demand to anyone they select within their supply chain. Payments are immediately available and are less expensive to process, allowing for smaller and more frequent orders to be placed, thus reducing inventory levels while increasing customer service levels.

Radio-Frequency Identification (RFID)

The use of bar codes was a great advancement for the logistics industry. It significantly reduced errors in warehousing processes. When RFID became available for application in most industries, the expected advantages were exciting. With RFID, in its most sophisticated form, it is possible for a two-way conversation between the tag and the receiver. Thus it allows for a close monitoring of the geographical position of the goods alongside the supply chain. RFID does not only reduce registering errors, but also highlights the process where opportunities for improvement lie. For instance, RFID can register information about delays of goods in a particular warehouse, such as at customs or at the transportation company. The adoption of RFID has been so significant that some suppliers like Walmart, for instance, do not buy from suppliers that cannot deliver RFID-tagged goods.

Smart Devices With GPS Capabilities

The previous advances in digital technology affected fundamentally the supply side. However, consumers' massive use of smart devices coupled with peoples' obsession to share their lives on social media has affected the side of demand providing logistics and marketing managers with information of incredible value. It is now possible to know not only where customers are, almost all the time, but what kind of products or services grabbed their attention, either by looking at the pages they visit on the Internet or just by following their comments on social media. Marketers have reacted to this very rich information by placing customized advertising on social media (e.g., on Facebook walls), with the expectation to match customers' needs and wants with value offerings. However, as GPS has limitations on geographical position accuracy, it does not work properly if people are indoors. For instance, in a shopping mall, the immediacy of marketing communication is not perfect, thus more suitable positioning devices need to be developed.

Beacons

Beacons are small, low-cost pieces of software with Bluetooth communication capabilities that solve the problems of GPS communication indoors. Beacons could be used to prompt customers' action in the precise moment that they are passing close to an offering marketers aim to grab their attention toward. A beacon is capable of figuring out where a customer is standing with great precision. Thus marketers are able to send a notification in the very precise moment that a person is passing by the front door of a store, for instance, and invite the customer to visit a particular aisle where a product is on sale, or to grab the attention of customers toward new arrivals and so on. The only requirement is that the customer downloads an App on her phone. The software that controls promotions is rather simple to use and marketers can experiment with different offerings to gain consumers' preference.

Mixed Reality

Mixed reality, sometimes referred to as hybrid reality, is the merging of real and virtual worlds to produce new environments and visualizations where physical and digital objects co-exist and interact in real time. Mixed reality takes place not only in the physical world or the virtual world, but is a mix of reality and virtual reality, encompassing both augmented reality and augmented virtuality via immersive technology.

One of the most amazing features of digital technology is the ability to use and interconnect extensive databases. Through mixed reality it is possible to overlap a number of layers of information that increase the quality of the communication means. For instance, a billboard in the past only had the ability to display a picture with very little text on it. Today it could become alive if viewed through the lenses of a smartphone. To illustrate, if the billboard were a picture of a car, the potential customer could almost experience the sensations of traveling in the car thanks to augmented reality technology. A 3D hologram announcing the presentation of a band could make the band start playing on a miniature stage and see the performers as 3D holograms and the viewer will connect his phone to the hologram to access information of the venue, pricing, and even to buy tickets for the concert. Moreover, the device will recognize the user and make suggestions or show customized content (Soto 2017). This way, marketing managers have the ability to convert passive communication offerings into vivid experiences for customers while increasing the effectiveness of the advertising by generating the sale.

Drones and Self-Driving Delivery Vehicles

With better information and, eventually, more appropriate communication strategies, customers become more motivated to purchase. However, their levels of tolerance regarding delivery time and failure also decreased. Thus, on the one hand advances in digital technology improved marketers' ability to attract customers, but on the other hand customers now expect higher levels of service. Marketers and logistics managers are very aware of the inefficiencies of transportation particularly at the last mile, with significant numbers of small vans delivering small parcels to end consumers with increased possibilities of being late and deliver to the wrong address. Last mile delivery is also very expensive, compared to the costs of consolidated shipping. Then, under the leadership of Amazon. com drones and self-driving delivery vehicles became a potential solution to the problem, with the expectation of lesser human intervention and therefore increased accuracy and immediacy. Drones are capable of flying distances long enough to replace couriers and autonomous cars can deliver inside towns. Although drones and autonomous cars will not be a complete substitute, their use increases the ability for logistics managers to fulfill delivery promises more efficiently.

The Internet of Things

IoT is the name given to a myriad of electronic artifacts connected to one another on the Internet. IoT is a powerful marketing tool as it collects information from customers' activities in several points at the moment of occurrence while allowing for interaction between people and products, making offerings go beyond traditional capabilities of products, and creating greater value for customers. The usefulness of IoT for marketing logistics managers is undeniable. However, one of its caveats is that the amount of data generated becomes excessive for the use of traditional data management tools, requiring not only increased computational power but also very sophisticated methods of data analysis.

In sum, digital technology has advanced businesses in a multitude of ways : abilities to react to customers' needs more efficiently, to understand customers' behavior better, to increase the efficiency of communication strategies by delivering the right message at the right moment, by increasing the vividness of the offering by putting together several layers of information, by facilitating the purchasing processes of customers, and by improving delivery processes, all in a world of interconnected people and products. However, digital technology has also increased customers' expectations of great service levels, made the world look smaller, and started data proliferation that common individuals using traditional tools cannot make sense of. Thus, the digital revolution opened the doors for further development of AI in order to take advantage of the immense amount of information available and the new customers' ability to interact with business directly.

Conversational interfaces, engagement platforms, big data, and machine learning systems are not only processes enabled by digital technology, but are the foundation of an intelligence platform.

Machine Learning

Machine learning is an application of AI that builds algorithmic systems based on previous data trends, models, and patterns that it has learned from. With this data, machine learning simulates the human decision-making process by using predictive analysis.

Experts believe that machine learning will continue to grow across all market spaces, acquiring an even larger presence within applications, digital assistants, and AI as a whole, including the drone and self-driving cars territory.

Artificial Intelligence

According to the latest Gartner research, by 2020, 85 percent of customer interactions will be managed by AI. Researchers predict AI will outperform humans in many activities in the next 10 years, such as translating languages (by 2024), writing high-school essays (by 2026), driving a truck (by 2027), working in retail (by 2031), writing a bestselling book (by 2049), and working as a surgeon (by 2053). The respondents believe there is a 50 percent chance of AI outperforming humans in all tasks in 45 years and of automating all human jobs in 120 years (Grace et al. 2017).

Artificial intelligence (AI) expands at a very fast pace; dynamics or developments in one sector or technology can influence another. Opportunities for multidisciplinary collaboration or risk mitigation are coalescing. The very definition of digital transformation is evolving. As of today, there is rapid development in algorithmic news stories, autonomous robotics, product recommendations, processing patient data, virtual assistants with voice recognition and far beyond, such that AI is slowly infusing all manner of industry, society, and life. Moreover, blockchain[1] will allow to share and use the AI technology in a secure and trusted way through "smart contracts."[2] In the future, AI will be integrated to marketing and logistics creating not only smart sales channels, but also customer support channels.

The Future: The Smart Logistics and Marketing Ecosystem

The future of marketing and logistics goes hand to hand with: location-based services, cloud computing, big data, mobile devices, IoT, robotics, autonomous vehicles, drones and smart carts, smart agents, machine learning algorithms, conversational interfaces, and engagement platforms. All these are creating a disruptive environment where all the

---

[1] Blockchain is a technology that holds information on a shared and continually reconciled database.

[2] Smart contract is an agreement that is linked into the code of a platform, so it automatically executes when the terms have been met, virtually eliminating counterparty risks and the need for middlemen.

magic is starting to work. Things, places, devices, smartphones, and business will all be smart agents in this new paradigm. Location intelligence, machine learning, IoT, and big data become the basis for the allocation of goods and contextual marketing in an AI-governed world.

The Smart Marketing Logistics Framework

The logistics and marketing ecosystem illustrated in Figure 8.1 becomes the smart logistics and marketing ecosystem when AI is merged with existing processes and products. In this new scenario, a framework will emerge that holds all processes of interaction driven by multiple actors that include marketers, logistics managers, suppliers of products and services, and overall customers, all operating in a highly connected interdependent network.

The smart marketing logistics framework, see Figure 8.2, runs applications for sales, marketing, customer service, operations, legal, finance, human resource, information technology (IT), supply chain, merchandising, logistics, and research and development (R&D). Marketing and logistics will become an integrated system to fulfill customer needs and make JIT a reality to improve factories and suppliers.

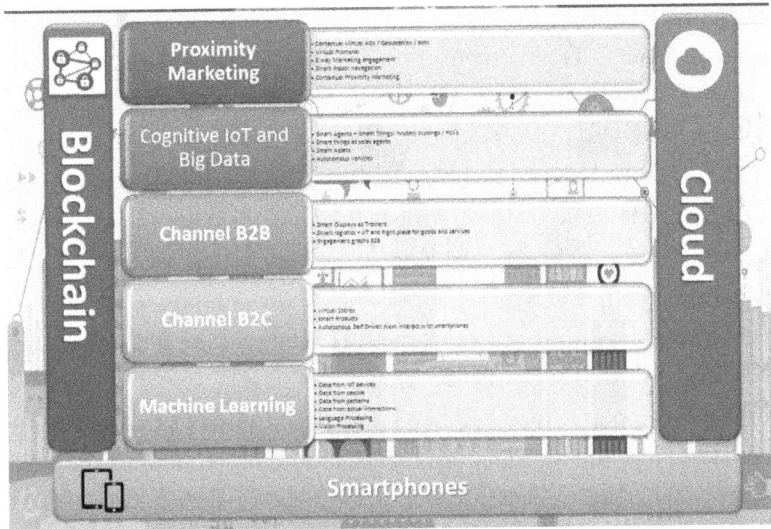

Figure 8.2 The smart marketing logistics framework

Foundations

The framework is a mesh of intelligent connected products as a result of AI (machine learning), cognitive IoT (big data, vision, and language), and blockchain (compliance and security) integration running in a smart cloud infrastructure. The key to this world are the smartphones with blockchain-based identity management system capable of securely exchanging information with smart devices (Newton 2017).

The Framework

The framework runs in the cloud and uses blockchain as a basis for security and trust, and the smartphones are the agents empowered by blockchain's digital ID systems. It is built on a stack of smart technologies and interactions like a mesh or engagement graph.

The components of the smart marketing logistics framework include: (1) proximity marketing, where elements are contextual virtual advertisments/geolocation/bots, Virtual Promoter, two-way marketing engagement, smart indoor navigation, contextual proximity marketing, (2) cognitive IoT and big data, where elements are smart agents—smart things/houses/buildings/points of information, smart things as sales agents, smart assets, autonomous vehicles, smart wallets, (3) channel B2B, where elements are blockchain digital ID, smart displays as trainers, smart logistics—JIT and right place for goods and services, engagement graphs B2B, (4) channel B2C, where elements are blockchain digital ID, virtual stores, smart products, autonomous self-driven kiosk, smart wallets in smartphones, and (5) machine learning, where elements are data from IoT devices, data from people, data from patterns, data from actual interactions, language processing, and vision processing.

Based on the framework, there is a new ecosystem: the smart logistics and marketing ecosystem (see Figure 8.1), where all the transactions are governed by AI. The marketing process and logistic act as one system driven by a holistic approach like humans do. Marketing decisions are based on machine learning algorithms that process location, profiles, supply chain data, human behavior, visual and textual analysis. The security and trust is in a blockchain network.

The warehouses as well as point of sales are managed by smart agents and robotics. Inside the stores most are smart devices capable of assisting the customers and marketing itself. Smart carts engaged with smartphones will be acting as virtual shoppers. The warehouses manage a fleet of autonomous vehicles and drones for the last mile.

The appliances are connected and interact with the suppliers to buy or request support and are capable of making suggestions to the users for new products or promotions.

Conclusion

AI might not be very new in the computer science arena. However, it is causing massive changes to the business environment, particularly in the intersection between marketing, logistics, and markets—where customers are found. AI has found fertile grounds in marketing logistics due to the strong infusion of digital technology to processes and devices that affected the flows of information, payments, and products. It also impacts customers' behavior, with the subsequent effect of creating enormous amounts of data, with analysis beyond the capabilities of individuals using conventional data management knowledge. AI disrupted the environment by challenging the validity of existing processes, and by creating new forms of interaction between customers and suppliers, where many tasks otherwise performed by humans were overtaken by machines. The future seems to be on the one hand somber, as humans appear to be made redundant. However, it could on the other hand be promising when human intelligence and abilities are devoted to more complex tasks beyond the abilities of AI that only the human brains are capable to deal with, thus allowing AI to govern marketing and logistics system ultimately for the benefit of human beings.

References

American Marketing Asociation 2013. "Marketing Definition." Retrieved from https://.ama.org/AboutAMA/Pages/Definition-of-Marketing.aspx

Grace, K., J. Salvatier, A. Dafoe, B. Zhang, and O. Evans. 2017. "When Will AI Exceed Human Performance?" *Evidence from AI Experts.*

Lummus, R.R., D.W. Krumwiede, and R.J. Vokurka. 2001. "The Relationship of Logistics to Supply Chain Management: Developing a Common Industry Definition." *Industrial Management & Data Systems* 101, no. 8, pp. 426–32.

Newton, P. 2017. "What Blockchain Means for the Sharing Economy." https://hbr.org/2017/03/what-blockchain-means-for-the-sharing-economy

Orwell, G. 1949. *Nineteen Eighty-Four.* New York, NY: Harcourt Brace.

Soto, L.A. 2017. "Tips Promotions, Smart Holograms, Dacorp SRL." http://tipspromotion.com

Wood, D.F. 1998. "Logistics." https://.britannica.com/topic/logistics-business#ref528537

CHAPTER 9

Artificial Intelligence and Customer Service in Health Care

Norrie J. Daroga

This chapter explores the intersection of AI, natural language processing, and speech recognition technologies to create a trusted virtual character. These virtual custom assistants (VCA) can provide consistent customer service to health care consumers, and, more importantly, *when* they need it.

Traditional customer service in health care is marred by inaccurate or incomplete information, inconsistent behavior of call center representatives, difficulty in predicting volume of calls and resultant staffing issues, and a high cost of human-to-human interaction for routine questions. For some demographics, mainly under age 35, the lack of a self-directed customer journey is essentially a poor customer experience. As cited in his article "Improving Health Outcomes with Better Patient Understanding and Education," Robert John Adams (2010) states: "for individuals to realize the benefits of health education also requires a high level of engagement ... Interventions to improve self-care have shown improvements in self-efficacy, patient satisfaction, coping skills, and perceptions of social support."

Enter an intelligent virtual character. Unlike chatbots, which are voice-only, task-oriented characters, an intelligent virtual character has a humanistic form, can be animated in 3D, understands the intent of the consumer, and can access a large library of relevant content. It can be voice activated, text, or both and is conversational rather than task-oriented. It is also contextual in its knowledge, and not suited for random interactions on a variety of topics, the way Siri and Cortana were designed.

Technology

Health care insurers have complex websites that attempt to answer frequently asked questions, allow customers to file claims, request replacement insurance cards, and perform a host of activities. Some are designed better than others, but in the end a large percentage of visitors to the website either use chatbots or call a human to achieve their desired result. Why? It's not the answer to the first question that matters, it's the ability to ask a follow-up question where the websites fail to satisfy the needs of the customer. It is the *conversation* that is ultimately missing.

Today, intelligent virtual characters have a combination of technologies that have reached a level of sophistication that allow people to have detailed conversations with them. It begins with automated speech recognition ("ASR") and text-to-speech ("TTS") engines, which are used to recognize the spoken words and reply with speech. The next technology is natural language processing ("NLP"), which provides context to the speech so that the *intent* of the customer is recognized. Some words sound the same, and others have the same spelling, but in each case their use in a sentence can have different meanings. NLP helps keep the conversation on track.

Next is emotion detection. While personality traits may be helpful in extended conversations and relationships, understanding the immediate mood of the customer is essential in customer service. Several software engines use micro-facial detection, tone of voice, choice of words or a combination of these clues to detect the mood of the customer, and the *changes* in mood as the conversation progresses. The mood then determines the response from the intelligent virtual character as well as the animation that characterizes an appropriate physical response. In an article, Milliard (2017) quoted Anthony Chambers, director in the life sciences practice at the Chicago-based consultancy West Monroe Partners, in an interview with *Healthcare IT News*:

If we could use an interactive bot, where the patient then has a point of conversation via smartphone or something, that could be a game changer because of the challenge of clinical trials being so stressful on the population, and the expense of running the trials. What gets really fascinating—we have yet to see it, but we're seeing discussions of it—is potential uses around the quality of care. That remains an untapped potential where the promise of emotional intelligence, in combination with AI, could play out.

How does artificial intelligence ("AI") fit in? AI, as a term of art, has lost its definition as companies try to market their products as having AI incorporated in them. In this chapter, AI is used to describe the software on a device, which allows the device to recognize *unstructured* data, such as a text, pictures, or videos, as input from a customer, and provide similar data to the customer in response to the input. For example, a table of frequently asked questions may try to recognize key words of text and match many answers from a database containing the same words. Some answers will be relevant, many may not. On the other hand, AI allows the customer to "speak" to the device in any number of ways, and the device "understands" the intent of the question and provides a highly contextual answer that it has been "trained" to provide. The device then verifies if the answer is satisfactory to the customer and, if not, goes to the next answer. Over time, AI determines the probability of the correct answer and refines the sequence of answers it provides over time. In essence, the process of understanding and responding mimics that of a human being answering the question, albeit in a more consistent and highly scalable manner. Virtual reality and AI are becoming an integral part of nursing. An article by Ferguson et al. (2016) in the *Contemporary Nurse Journal* stated: "These technologies can be utilized in many settings to assist in health behavior change interventions, optimize care, and improve health outcomes of individuals across all care settings."

AI also offers the opportunity for a follow-up question on the answer presented by the virtual character, an essential element to ensuring a high quality of customer service. There are numerous AI engines available, and most utilize application programming interfaces ("APIs") to enable developers to quickly create software programs using the AI capability. The bulk of the work these days is in training the AI to be conversational in its interaction, and an ecosystem has been built around companies that help with this process, like companies that assist in integrating medical records into an electronic medical record ("EMR") system.

AI is often incorrectly used interchangeably with deep machine learning, which is an advanced form of analytic and predictive software with neural networks, which is the science of nonlinear machine processing also used in pattern prediction. This chapter is limited to technology that enables a device to listen to a person and respond by voice or text to answer a question.

Health care is one of the few industries where the customer is an indirect payer for services received. Pricing for the services is rarely transparent, and the quality of the provider is hard to determine before receiving the services. In health care, consumers often speak with call center representatives and, for the purposes of this chapter, the experience is separated by (i) customer acquisition and (ii) cost reduction.

Customer Acquisition/Retention

All large health care payers, providers, and physician practices have a website; some are elaborate and others are rudimentary. The purpose of the website may vary from merely creating a presence with information about services and locations, to allowing a user to perform transactions, obtain health care test results, and customize the experience. Once developed, it is rare for the design to be revised over several years, with content creation being the only activity devoted to its maintenance. The initial cost of development may be a few thousand or several hundred thousand dollars, but very few are developed with user experience at the center of the design effort. The technology described above enables the implementation of a digital character (agent/advisor/avatar/assistant or some variant is used by numerous vendors), that can guide a user through an engaging experience.

Open Enrollment for Insurance Plans

Selection of an insurance plan can be a daunting task. An avatar leads you to the plan selection page, where graphical sliders allow you to adjust the deductibles, network flexibility, and monthly premiums. Based on the user's selection of these sliders, the avatar identifies plans that meet these criteria and displays the availability of Health Savings Account (HAS) and employer-match options for such plans. The user can ask questions about a specific plan, by voice or by text, and get answers from content approved by the insurers' risk management group. The content may include text or video format and the user can leave the website and resume the interaction, just as one would with a Digital Video Recorder (DVR). Plans can be compared side-by-side as the user explores various options.

Once a plan is selected, the avatar pre-populates any required forms (if the user is already a member who selects a different plan or changes participant coverage) or assists the user in entering the required information for a new member. At the end of the guided experience, the user is enrolled as a member without having any direct interaction with a call center associate.

The metrics for use of an avatar-based open enrollment experience are compelling:

- 87 percent pull through of users to completion of enrollment
- 90 percent increase in accuracy of completed forms
- 33 percent reduction in labor costs of call center operations

The next generation of interaction will allow an existing member to select a plan based on the member's historical claims data, use of specific providers, customer satisfaction scores for providers, pharmacy usage, and other content from the insurer that is made available during the guided experience. This level of personalization will allow the member to select plans that are outcome-based, providing the insurer with a "customer-for-life" opportunity in customer service.

Cost Reduction

According to the Center for Disease Control and Prevention (2017), over 75 percent of the cost of health care in the United States is driven by chronic diseases. There are 22 chronic diseases, of which the top five account for 80 percent of the cost of chronic diseases. In general, the treatment of chronic diseases is episodic, similar to the treatment of acute health issues. However, management of chronic diseases requires care coordination, symptom management, and behavior modification to reduce the cost associated with managing the disease. Ward et al. (2014) indicated in a report titled *Multiple Chronic Conditions among US Adults: A 2012 Update* that

> Other factors, such as medication compliance and use of urgent care, also pay a large role in these costs. Some of the primary goals of the national CDC initiative focused on addressing multiple chronic conditions in the United States include strengthening health care and public health systems, improving self-care management of [them], and providing better tools and information to health care providers.

Care coordination is currently a highly manual process, conducted by skilled labor such as nurses, physician assistants, and social workers. On average, a case manager is assigned over a thousand patients and spends a considerable amount of time measuring body vitals on patients, entering the data, tracking it, and responding to alerts generated when the data shows a patient to be outside normal ranges. Most patients end up in urgent care or emergency departments anyway, since the process is not scalable and the employee turnover tends to remain high among case managers. Collier, Fu, and Yin (2017) cited an Accenture study that stated:

> Growth opportunities are hard to come by without significant investment, but artificial intelligence (AI) is a self-running engine for growth in health care. When combined, key clinical health AI applications can potentially create $150 billion in annual savings for the US health care economy by 2026.

Chronic Disease Management

AI is particularly suited for this use case. A virtual assistant can be implemented to interact with the patient, either on demand or on a scheduled basis, to inquire about the patient's status on:

- Activities of daily living to determine ability to live independently

- ○ Eating, bathing, dressing, toileting, transferring (walking), and continence
- Mood
- Medication adherence
- Exercise levels
- Body vitals

This information can be collected without human intervention, and can be used to identify trends in the progression of the disease. The trending and daily information can be triaged based on medical best practices, and patients that need attention can be brought to the attention of the case manager. Now, instead of conducting data collection and analysis, the case manager performs triage and intervention, allowing the case manager to handle a much higher volume (2× to 5× in most cases) of patients, with better outcomes and lower cost of intervention. The patient feels empowered and engaged in management of their condition and over time, and the frequency and intensity of symptoms decrease through this approach, which cannot be effectively implemented without the use of AI-driven technology.

The development of medical-grade sensors by companies that traditionally focus on consumer products, such as the recently released Apple Watch, will allow machine-driven collection of body vitals in real time, further improving the quality of data and the frequency of collection to improve the analytics necessary to monitor the condition of patients with chronic diseases. Use of the virtual assistant will ensure patient engagement levels that in the past have eluded manufacturers of exercise devices/monitors, since the data collected now has relevance to the patient's health. The data will be more accurate than patient-reported data, since devices will communicate directly via Bluetooth or other emerging technologies.

Conclusions

Implementing AI in a clinical setting requires a thorough understanding of the workflow and processes currently in place in the departments likely to be affected by the technology, and a willingness to modify these processes to leverage the technology rather than using AI to incrementally improve existing processes. Here are four strategic areas that lend themselves to implementation of AI.

Case Management

The elderly population continues to increase as a percentage of the overall U.S. population, and adults over 50 years of age already have multiple chronic diseases. Congestive heart failure (CHF) and chronic obstructive pulmonary disease (COPD) are two of the top five chronic diseases in terms of prevalence and cost. The occurrence of symptoms often leads to emergency care and care for these patients is usually managed through intervention by nurses and case managers.

Studies show that intervention during early signs of symptoms saves a considerable amount of cost for these diseases. In the case of CHF, a weight gain of 2 pounds indicates a patient is likely to need urgent care in about 24 to 48 hours. For COPD, increased frequency of rescue inhalers is a sign that intervention in a clinical setting will be necessary in short order. Hospital systems employ thousands of case managers to reach out to patients and monitor these trends; communication usually is by telephone and may include texts and e-mails. Response from patients varies greatly and case managers have a high rate of burnout in their jobs.

Enter a virtual assistant powered by AI. The hospital provides the patient with a dedicated device, generally a tablet, preloaded with the assistant, along with sensors to measure body vitals. Each day, at a time convenient for the patient, the assistant engages the patient by asking a few questions and then measuring body vitals that are related to the disease. The sensors communicate to the virtual assistant in real time through Bluetooth. Once the measurements are completed, the information is transmitted to the case manager in a report format. Each patient has metrics assigned, and trend data as well as variations from prescribed values alerts the case manager when a patient needs intervention. By focusing only on patients that need attention, the case manager can manage over 2,500 patients, a 5× increase from current standards, while providing far better care to those patients who need it. In his article titled "Market Insight: How Service Providers' Strategic Planners Should Target the Remote Patient Monitoring Market," Gupta (2016) argues that

Remote patient monitoring offers the potential to deliver hospital-grade monitoring outside of the care setting. Strategic planners need to understand why RPM is being discussed now, where the main growth segments are and what to know to effectively position their offerings in this market.

Patient Portal

Most health systems and their physician practices have patient portals, where secure access is given to the patient for lab results, appointments, and physician notes from the patient's records. Its purpose is to provide a self-directed experience for the patient to obtain information at their own pace and on their own time. The portals are poorly designed without the user experience in mind, and the patient ends up calling the doctor's office to speak to a nurse. If the patient has questions about the meaning of the test results, the nurse generally schedules a conversation between the doctor and the patient.

A virtual assistant with AI can substantially reduce the burden for doctors and their staff. It can notify the patient when the results are posted on the patient portal, identify any abnormalities and provide context around the variations, identify the need and type of follow-up necessary, and schedule the subsequent appointments, all without interaction with the nurse or doctor. It does this conversationally, just like the patient would experience with a person, and has content that allows it to answer questions consistently and repeatedly, without judgment and without irritation. Specialists within the health care system get automatic referrals and can even prioritize calendaring based on the patient's condition.

Primary Care

Access to primary care and subsequent treatment is another major cost factor in health care. Pharmacies now have clinics, the Internet provides millions of resources to self-diagnose, and call centers staffed with doctors are available to prescribe medications. Ride-sharing services are available to take patients to clinics and concierge medicine is on the rise.

In most cases, the symptoms that require primary care are straightforward and the diagnosis is fairly consistent. AI allows a patient to describe symptoms to a virtual assistant, and the virtual assistant can clarify the symptoms by asking the patient questions, much like a nurse would. Using specific algorithms to perform a differential analysis, the virtual assistant sends the information to a nurse or doctor at a remote location along with suggestions of the likely diagnosis; the doctor or nurse reviews the information, verifies the diagnosis, and prescribes medication or suggests an office visit, handling substantially higher volumes of patients than possible if the patient was having a direct conversation with the doctor or nurse.

OTC Drug Interaction

A substantial number of drugs dispensed in the United States are nonprescribed. This includes drugs that formerly required prescriptions but are now available over-the-counter (OTC). Pain relievers and allergy medication are two of the more prevalent types of drugs in this category. When pharmacists dispense drugs, they are likely to watch for drug interactions, proper dosage, and other conditions that may affect the patient. They have access to databases that provide them with necessary information. Once the drug is an OTC drug, however, the consumer is on their own. Labels on the medication can be confusing and often similar in appearance between the different strengths of the drug. Taking 10 mg of a drug instead of 1 mg can have disastrous effect on the consumer.

Using a device such as a smartphone, an app can access the same information available to the pharmacist and alert the consumer on possible contraindications. The camera on the smartphone can scan the code on the product and compare it to medical information previously entered by the consumer. The interaction can be conversational right at the point of sale, and can even commence with a recommended dosage and list active ingredients before the consumer goes to the pharmacy.

The current political debate has focused on how to pay for health care in the United States; the real issue is the high cost of care, the inconsistency among providers in the outcomes, and disintermediation of the patient—physician relationship. Iuga and McGuire (2014) of Johns

Hopkins Bloomberg School of Public Health state in *Adherence and Heath Care Costs* that

> In 2010 the costs of health care in the US exceeded $2.7 trillion and accounted for 17.9 percent of the gross domestic product. Projections indicate health care will account for 20 percent of the US gross domestic product by 2020. Twenty percent to 30 percent of dollars spent in the US health care system have been identified as wasteful. Providers and administrators have been challenged to contain costs by reducing waste and by improving the effectiveness of care delivered.

The use of AI technologies will result in a revised model of health care in the United States and many parts of the developing world, by increasing patient satisfaction and levels of engagement in their own health, early symptom tracking, outcome-based care models, and continuous monitoring of chronic diseases. However, the real advantage will be improved quality of life for patients and satisfaction among health care professionals on a job well done!

References

Adams, R.J. 2010. "Improving Health Outcomes with Better Patient Understanding and Education." *Risk Management and Healthcare Policy.* Viewable at https://.ncbi.nlm.nih.gov/pmc/articles/PMC3270921/ (accessed October 14, 2010).

Center for Disease Control and Prevention. 2017. "Preventive Health Care, what's the problem?" *Center for Disease Control and Prevention.* Viewable at https://.cdc.gov/healthcommunication/toolstemplates/entertainmented/tips/PreventiveHealth.html (accessed September 15, 2017).

Collier, M., R. Fu, and L. Yin. 2017. "Artificial Intelligence: Healthcare's New Nervous System." *AI Thinks and Pays for Itself, Anderson Consulting.* Viewable at https://.accenture.com/t20170418T023006Z__w__/us-en/_acnmedia/PDF-49/Accenture-Health-Artificial-Intelligence.pdf

Ferguson, C., P.M. Davidson, P.J. Scott, D. Jackson, and L.D. Hickman. 2016. "Augmented Reality, Virtual Reality and Gaming: an Integral Part of Nursing." *Contemporary Nurse,* Viewable at http://.tandfonline.com/doi/abs/10.1080/10376178.2015.1130360?journalCode=rcnj20 (accessed January 14, 2016).

Gupta A. 2016. "Market Insight: How Service Providers' Strategic Planners Should Target the Remote Patient Monitoring Market." *Gartner*, Viewable at https://.gartner.com/doc/3383517/market-insight-service-providers-strategic (accessed July 19, 2016).

Iuga, A.O., and M.J. McGuire. 2014. "Adherence and Health Care Costs." *Risk Management and Healthcare Policy*, Viewable at https://.ncbi.nlm.nih.gov/pmc/articles/PMC3934668/ (accessed February 14, 2014).

Miliard, M. 2017. "The Next Big Thing in AI, Emotional Intelligence, Could Give Hospitals a Competitive Edge." *Healthcare IT News*, Viewable at http://.healthcareitnews.com/news/next-big-thing-ai-emotional-intelligence-could-give-hospitals-competitive-edge (accessed August 17, 2017).

Ward, B.W., J.S. Schiller, and R.A. Goodman, 2014. "Multiple Chronic Conditions Among US Adults: A 2012 Update." *Preventing Chronic Disease*, Viewable at https://.cdc.gov/pcd/issues/2014/13_0389.htm (accessed April 17, 2014).

CHAPTER 10

Artificial Intelligence-Based Decision Making Applied in Marketing and Sales in Third World Countries

Abel Kinoti Meru, Felix Musau, and Mary Wanjiru Kinoti

Introduction

Techonomy is quickly changing the way of doing business worldwide, both sectoralwise and within functional areas including business-to-business, business-to-consumer, or at person-to-person level with profound positive implications. This is especially true in third world countries, resulting in a paradigm shift in the provision of goods and services. The so dubbed everyone-to-everyone (E2E) economy is driven by business ecosystems that are collaborative and seamless, user-specific, symbiotic, and cognitive (Glass, Haller, Marshall, and Yoragupipati 2017). The E2E economy shifts the focus from institutional centricity to user centricity (Cheung, Marshall, and McCarty 2017) determined by the artificial intelligence (AI) technology. This is the cumulative effect of massive automation of government processes, public and private firm activities, the economic sector, coupled with use of cognitive analytics and AI over the last decade or so. This scenario is giving hope to billions of people in the third world economies, who previously relied on discrete or none existing business processes.

While traditional digital automation processes boosted storage, retrieval, and application of information data sources, cognitive analytics as per Abercombie, Ezry, Goehring, Marshall, and Nakayoma (2017) sifts through data to unlock meaning and make recommendations, since machines can understand unstructured information such as imagery, natural language, and sounds from books and social media among others. For instance, cognitive technology enables a machine to demonstrate human like intelligence, utilizing big data to make informed decisions, offer suggestions or direct action compared to use of programming codes (McKinsey Global Institute (MGI) 2017a).

This MGI (2017a) paper notes further that AI enables machines to identify multifaceted patterns, synthesize information, predict, and draw resolutions, which were previously the domain of human beings. Globally, tech giants like Amazon, Apple, Baidu, and Google are leading in the development of AI, with instances of outright buying or working with AI start-ups and keenly eyeing to cash in using artificial systems/agents. AI, if harnessed as a new factor of production, will definitely enhance labor productivity and sustain double-digit economic growth rates in many parts of the world (Purdy and Daugherty 2016), including third world countries.

Again, it is imperative to note that key foundation technologies of AI like use of cloud, mobile, and Internet of things (IoT) are positively correlated to the diffusion and adoption of AI technologies globally. The MGI (2017a) report rightly observes that AI adoption is correlated to the level of digitization. For instance, within the transport and logistics spectrum, which carries a huge burden in third world countries, it is observed that by 2030 new automotive technologies like car sharing, autonomous driving, and integrated transport transit infrastructure will be the norm (MGI 2017b).

AI has ripple effects on an enterprise's functional activities commencing with the back office (finance, human resources, IT, and procurement), through the middle office (innovation, production/operations, product development, risk management, and supply chain management) to the front office comprising mainly of customer service, marketing, and sales (Abercombie et al. 2017) activities, which is the focus of this chapter, with emphasis on third world countries. The rest of the chapter provides an overview of AI-based decision-making systems applied to marketing, sales, and customer service, and then the implications of AI in marketing and sales in third world countries are presented, followed by conclusion and recommendations for policy implications.

The AI-Based Decision-Making Systems Applied in Marketing and Sales

The highest AI growth sectors are in high tech and telecommunications, automotive and assembly, and financial services; then the middle sectors include resources and utilities, media and entertainment, consumer packaged goods, transport and logistics, retail, and professional services, while the lower adopters are in the education and health sectors (MGI 2017a). eMarketer (2015) analysis of digital advertising earnings found out that 55 percent of the revenues were driven by programmatic marketing activities due to speed of data processing and machine learning techniques, with projected increases of up to 63 percent.

Though there is no well-delineated subfields of AI globally, this chapter has adopted five sets of AI technology systems development areas: (1) computer vision, (2) natural language that is used to process external information, (3) machine learning (including deep learning) that learns from information provided, (4) robotics and autonomous vehicles, and (5) virtual agents that act on information (MGI 2017a). The report further shows that machine learning had attracted the highest investment of 60 percent in 2016, followed by computer vision at 30 percent. There were insignificant investments in natural language, smart robotics and autonomous vehicles, and virtual agents.

For instance, the retailing sector utilizes machine learning and robotics mainly in promotion, assortments, and supply chain, enabling smarter decisions and real-time forecasting (MGI 2017a). Cheung et al. (2017) further observe that AI has deeply changed consumer-centric enterprises by creating personalized customer experiences, in areas like personal care (Procter & Gamble's Olay brand analysis of mobile phone digital selfies to offer skin solutions) and food (Campbell soup uses location-based personalized recipes) among others. Also, wholesalers and retailers use AI to predict customer behaviors, analyze fast-moving goods, and integrate front-end and back-end office operations.

Evolution of AI in marketing and sales is creating opportunities for growth in public and private enterprises. Te, Tsai-Fong, and Chieh-Heng (2016) point emerging fields in AI and marketing, sales, and customer service such as marketing solutions, virtual customer service agents, automated marketing and sales, virtual assistants, and marketing decision making. AI in marketing can help process big data to identify target customers, utilize multichannel for marketing campaigns, conduct powerful research for market positioning, identify pattern of high-conversion propensities, and improve accuracy in reporting marketing activities (Abercombie et al. 2017).

Further, use of AI in sales function can eliminate front office/customer-facing services, improve key account management, enhance cross-sell and upsell prospects, and improve efficiency in lead time management (Abercombie et al. 2017). Zhou (2017) observes that AI can augment customer service experience first through front-end AI-powered bots like chatbox, automated responses to basic customer queries, and the drastic reduction of customer service cycle time. Second, the AI-assisted human agent or human loop supports human customer service representative through AI technology like the case of text and voice inquiries, where the AI platform initiates the response or vents callers and the customer care human representative makes the final reply.

The AI-Based Decision-Making Systems Applied in Marketing and Sales by the Association Of Southeast Asian Nations (ASEAN)

AI continues to impact all markets globally particularly in the marketing and sales field even with inherent differences in infrastructure and systems in third world countries. The MGI (2017) paper observes that AI investment in ASEAN had reached US$ 2.6 billion in 2016 driven by wide-ranging technologies such as natural language processing (Bindez, Myanmar; kata.ai, Indonesia; and FPT, Vietnam), machine learning (CloudSek, India, and Runngaru, Indonesia), and image recognition (Sero, Vietnam), led by high tech, telecommunication, and financial services industries.

The ASEAN telecommunication firms are using analytics to predict customer behavior, upsell or cross-sell, and offer mobile banking, insurance, and loans. For instance, Dataspark (Singtel) collects and analyzes shoppers' information, and Eureka (Indosat) concentrates on digital marketing for retailers and offers credit rating services to banks (MGI 2017a). Further, from the paper, the financial sector has over 300 FinTech start-ups offering payments, micro lending, and wealth management, and big firms such as Hong Leong Bank (Malaysia) are using IBM Watson to decipher customer voices over the phone. Digibank (Singapore) utilizes virtual assistant to respond to customer queries, and CompareAsiaGroup uses machine learning to match customer needs with financial, telecom, and utilities requirements in five ASEAN countries.

Within the manufacturing sector industry 4.0, digital transformation of the sector is driven by IoT, AI, robotics, and 3D printing thereby enabling motionless management of factory floors, value chain, seamless flow of information leading to real-time decisions, and production efficiency (MGI 2017a). For instance, in China, Alibaba has made inroads connecting cars to the Internet and slowly moving on to introduce cloud-based AI services aimed at health care and manufacturing sectors (Daugherty 2017b). According to the McKinsey Global Institute (2017a) paper, future prosperity in China will be determined by the rate of adoption of AI technologies to accelerate economic growth. This situation is replicated in most other ASEAN and Middle East countries, but the phase in Africa is certainly lower.

The AI-Based Decision-Making Systems Applied in Marketing and Sales in Africa

A similar pattern of application of AI globally in the key sectors of telecommunications, financial services, retail, transport, and logistics is evident in Africa, albeit on a smaller scale. This could be partly explained by the fact that AI is relatively young in the continent, poor infrastructure, and limited development of techonomy infrastructure and systems including skills and capabilities. Equally visible is the lack of government support to create an enabling environment such as policy framework, building public infrastructure and networks, and addressing cybersecurity issues.

There is also a general lack of preparedness and stakeholder involvement, thereby requiring private and international high tech and telecommunication firms to take a proactive role in the sector. All in all, the cost of doing business is prohibitive coupled with a dearth of AI-related skills and widespread illiteracy among the rural folks. It is also noteworthy that, although deeper inroads are visible, they are cluttered within the rural and urban areas and across regions.

Notable AI systems, although all are dependent on the telecommunication sector, include: M-Pesa and Pesapal (Kenya) in financial sector; in the retailing sector there is Jumia and Mall for Africa (Nigeria), SMSGH and Esoko (Ghana), and OLX (South Africa). In transport and logistics, Uber is present in a number of countries, Little Cab (Kenya), and Zebra and Jozibear (South Africa). In the agricultural sector, there is M-Farm (Kenya) and Farmerline (Ghana). A list is shown in Table 10.1.

From Table 10.1, it is clear that apart from the cash transfer services M-Pesa's micro savings and credit services such as M-Shwari analyzes customers' mobile usage, payment history, and credit rating among others to determine credit worthiness. Safaricom owns an innovation center to further develop an AI monetary platform to help analyze customer transaction history and to enable them make informed financial decisions (Bright 2017). Pesapal is an online and mobile payments system for individuals, businesses, and governments in Kenya (Pesapal 2017), akin to Safaricom but with limited scope.

Ushahidi gathers and analyzes information from disaster zones through SMS, E-mails, WhtatsApp, Webapp, and Twitter and shares simultaneously with disaster management units on a real-time basis. M-Farm was created in 2009 to mitigate agriculture-related risks, especially in the rural areas, and it enables farmers to source information easily, get inputs cheaply, and sell produce timely and competitively (Mfarm 2017), similar to Farmerline. Uber, an e-hailing taxi services, commenced operations in Kenya in January 2015, and since then numerous other apps are in operation including Taxify (Turkey) and rapid homegrown taxi e-hailing solutions like Little Ride, MaraMoja, and Dandia (Njanja 2016, p. 19). Little Ride is co-owned by Craft Silicon and Safaricom

Table 10.1 *Selected AI-based decision-making systems applied in marketing and sales in Africa*

Year	Digital innovation	Country	Functionality	AI capability	Source
2007	Safaricom-M-Pesa services	Kenya	Mobile money transfer/micro-savings and credit	Machine learning	Mureithi (2017)/Bright (2017)
2008	Ushahidi	Kenya	Crisis management	Machine learning	Mureithi (2017)
2009	M-Farm	Kenya	Connect farmers and buyers	Machine learning	Osikakwan (2017), MFarm (2017)
2009	Pesapal	Kenya	Payment aggregation platform	Machine learning	Osikakwan (2017)
2015	Uber	Kenya	Integrated convenient travel and pay solutions	Machine learning	Biznews (2017)
2016	Little Cab	Kenya	Integrated convenient travel and pay solutions	Machine learning	Biznews (2017)
2012/2010	Jumia/Mall for Africa	Nigeria	Online shopping	Machine leaning	Osikakwan (2017)
2012/2004	Farmerline/Esoko	Ghana	e-Agriculture	Machine learning/natural language	Osikakwan (2017)
	SMSGH	Ghana	Communication, content, commerce	Machine learning	Osikakwan (2017)
	OLX	South Africa	Online shopping	Machine learning	Osikakwan (2017)
2013	Uber	South Africa	Integrated convenient travel and pay solutions	Machine learning	Biznews (2017)
2016	Zebra cabs/Jozibear	South Africa	Integrated convenient travel and pay solutions	Machine learning	Biznews (2017)

Source: Author's own from literature (2017).

telecommunication firm, and comes with free wifi, mobile money payment mechanism, ride sharing, loyalty scheme, lady drivers, corporate taxi, and a feedback mechanism.

Online shopping is dominated by Jumia, found in Nigeria and a dozen African countries (Jumia 2017), while Esoko is found in Ghana. Mall for Africa connects African online retailers with their counterparts in the United States and Europe (Mall for Africa 2017).

Conclusion

As the global digital economy evolves fundamental changes especially in the field of marketing and sales will redefine tomorrow's business operations. It is evident that AI will take central stage in bifurcating the human and machine interfaces. While the U.S. market has the first mover advantage, the strides made by China, ASEAN firms, and inroads by African companies cannot be taken for granted. Advances made by China, Singapore, India, Malaysia, Vietnam, Nigeria, Kenya, Ghana, and South Africa are worth paying attention to. Absolute transformation is being witnessed in the telecommunication, financial services, transport and logistics, agriculture, health, and media sectors in the third world countries.

Despite the gains, there are a couple of issues related to labor markets, regulatory framework, market dominance, cost of technology systems, and cybersecurity that beg answers. Already in the banking sector, banks are closing branches and laying off staff as a result of mobile money transfers. The same is observed in other sectors, so the question of employment will need to be carefully assessed since a large proportion of the population relies on wages and salaries, and they constitute a sizeable consumer market. Economies in the third world countries thrive mainly on taxes, but techonomy is borderless and creates a myriad of challenges with relevant tax authorities. Mobile money transfer, though somehow regulated by central banks, works mostly in the microlevel or even peer-to-peer lending, making it extremely difficult to regulate.

The growth and dominance of Uber hailing taxi services in different parts of the world left many players astounded. There are instances, where they thrived without legal approvals, stakeholder consultation, or an explanation of the business model, resulting in resistance, huge fines, and penalties. The cost of Internet and other related technology infrastructure seems a real threat to the growth and development of techonomy in the third world countries. Like any other public mega infrastructure, the cost should be borne absolutely by the governments. However, this has been left to profiteers at the expense of the taxpayers. Finally, the issue of cybersecurity is posing a great threat to the growth of the sector, since like in the banking industry there are incidences of massive fraud by hackers. Moreover, the issue of what happens if the system fails is disturbing.

Recommendations

It is evident that AI if properly harnessed will substantially contribute to the socioeconomic development of third world countries through innovative and inclusive marketing and sales models with the ability to serve marginalized communities. However, for this to happen, issues of the job market, regulatory framework, market dominance, cost of technology systems, and cybersecurity ought to be addressed once and for all. The issue of the effect of IT on the labor workforce, as discussed at length, has no tangible answers. But, what is imminent is that firms are getting leaner day by day. Since the interaction between human and machines will remain forever, there is need for equipping human beings with the requisite skills needed in the AI sector.

These skills should empower human beings to fully understand computer visioning, natural machine learning (including deep learning) robotics, autonomous vehicles, virtual agents, and industry 4.0 techniques (IoT and 3D printing). Third world governments need to play a fundamental active role in creating an enabling environment by enacting appropriate techonomy laws and policies, and building a pool of talents with requisite skills from universities, polytechnics, and AI incubators in all fields, located in various parts of the world. Governments will also need to develop regional AI protocols and agreements to guide virtual growth of the sector.

Finally, the cost of doing business in the techonomy era, if not properly controlled, could be life-threatening, simply because like air there is no life without Internet. It is difficult to communicate with others in far-flung and remote areas with no Internet. The people have fully embraced E-mails, WhatsApp, chatbox, and so on as means of communication. Therefore, governments in third world countries, needs to prioritize investments in information technology to grow the techonomy, besides addressing the increased need for embracing AI into marketing and sales.

References

Abercombie, C., R. Ezry, B. Goehring, A. Marshall, and H. Nakayoma. 2017. "Accelerating Enterprise Reinvention: How to Build a Cognitive Organization." *IBM Institute of Value Chain.* https://-01.ibm.com/common/ssi/cgibin/ssialias?htmlfid (accessed October 22, 2017).

Artificial Intelligence and Robotics and their Workplace. https://.google.com/search?q=artificial+intelligence+in+developing+countries&oq=artificial+intelligence+in+developing+&gs (accessed October 20, 2017).

Biznews. 2017. "High Tech Taxi—Cab Hailing in Africa—a Tale of Two Countries." https://.biznews.com/africa/2017/03/14/taxi-cab-uber-kenya-sa/ (accessed October 23, 2017).

Bright, J. 2017. "Safaricom Launches Innovation Center to Move Beyond Mpesa." https://techcrunch.com/2017/10/18/safaricom-launches-innovation-center-to-move-beyond-m-pesa/?ncid=rss (accessed October 23, 2017).

Burtner, K., L. Dave, and H. Grace. 2017. "The Human Machine Interchange: How Intelligent Automation is Changing the way Business Operates." *IBM Institute of Value Chain.* https://public.dhe.ibm.com/common/ssi/ecm/gb/en/gbe03879usen/the-human-machine-interchange.pdf (accessed October 22, 2017).

Cheung, J., A. Marshall, and D. McCarty. 2017. "Realising the Future of Today: Digital Revolution in Cosumer Products." https:// 935.ibm.com/services/us/gbs/thoughtleadership/drcp/ (accessed October 22, 2017).

Daugherty, P. 2017a. "The changing face of business and the part AL has to play." www.weforum.org/agenda/2016/12/how-artificial-intelligence-could-change-the-face-of-business (accessed October 22, 2017).

Daugherty, P. 2017b. "How China became an AI leader" https://.weforum.org/agenda/2017/06/how-china-became-ai-leader/ (accessed October 16, 2017).

Edgeverve. 2016. "Artificial Intelligence to Drive Future of Innovation." https://.edgeverve.com/wp-content/uploads/2016/11/ai-drive-future-innovation.pdf (accessed October 16, 2017).

eMarketer. 2017. "Artificial Intelligence: What's Now, What's New and What's Next." www.emarketer.com (downloaded October 17, 2017).

Glass, S., K. Haller, A. Marshall, and S.K. Yoragupipati. 2017. "Leading from the Front. Digital Reinvention in Retail." *IBM Institute of Value Chain*. https://www-935.ibm.com/services/us/gbs/thoughtleadership/drretail/ (accessed October, 22, 2017).

Hall, C. 1992. "Neural Net Technology—Ready for Prime-Time." *IEEE Expert* 7, no. 6, pp. 2–4.

Jumia. 2017. "Leading Online Shopping." https://.jumia.com.ng/ (retrieved October 21, 2017).

Mall for Africa. 2017. "E-commerce in Africa." www.mallforafrica.com. (retrieved October 22, 2017).

Mckinsey Global Institute. 2017a. "Artificial Intellingence The Next Digital Frontier?" Discussion Paper, April, 2017. https://.google.com/search?q=Artificial+Intellingence+the+next+digital+frontier%3F+Discussion+paper%2C+June%2C+2017&oq=Artificial+Intellingence+the+next+digital+frontier%3F+Discussion+paper%2C+June%2C+2017&aqs=chrome..69i57.3205j0j7&sourceid=chrome&ie=UTF-8 (accessed October 22, 2017).

Mckinsey Global Institute. 2017b. "Artificial Intellingence and South East Asia's Future." https://.mckinsey.com/~/media/McKinsey/Global%20Themes/Artificial%20Intelligence/Artificial-intelligence-and-Southeast-Asias-future.ashx (accessed October 20, 2017).

MFarm. 2017. "Ag—Risk Management." http://agriskmanagementforum.org/content/basic-concepts (accessed October 23, 2017).

Mureithi, M. 2017. "The Internet Journey of Kenya: The Interplay of Disruptive Innovation and Entrepreneurialship in Funding Rapid Growth." In *Digital Kenya: An Entrepreneurial Revolution in the Making,* eds. B. Ndemo and T. Weiss. London: Palgrave Macmillan.

Njanja, A. 2016. "Battle for e-hailing Market Share moves to Personalized Services." *Business Daily*, October 19. http://.businessdailyafrica.com/Battle-for-Kenya-e-hailing-market-share-moves-to-services/1248928-3422624-o2152w/index.html/ (retrieved October 6, 2017).

Osikakwan, E.M.K. 2017. "The Kings of Africa's Digital Economy." In *Digital Kenya: An Entrepreneurial Revolution in the Making,* eds. B. Ndemo and T. Weiss. London: Palgrave Macmillan.

Pesapal. 2017. "Pay, Shop and Receive Payment-Kenya." https://.google.com/search?q=pesa+pal&oq=pesa+pal&aqs=chrome..69i57.4311j0j9&sourceid=chrome&ie=UTF-8 (retrieved October 22, 2017).

Purdy, M., and P. Daugherty. 2016. "Why AI I sthe Future of Growth. Accenture." https://.accenture.com/lv-en/_acnmedia/PDF-33/Accenture-Why-AI-is-the-Future-of-Growth.pdf (accessed October 15, 2017).

Te, F., T. Tsai-Fong, and K. Chieh-Heng. 2016. "Application of Artificial Intelligence to cross-Screen Marketing: A Case Study of AI Technology Company," 2nd International Conference on Artificial Intelligence and Industrial Engineering (AIIE2016), Advances in Intelligent Systems Research.

Ushahidi. 2017. "Ushahidi for Crises Response." https://.ushahidi.com/ (accessed October 17, 2017).

Zhou, A. 2017. "How Artificial Intelliengence is Transforming Enterprise Customer Service." https://forbes.com/sites/adelynzhou/2017/02/27/how-artificial-intelligence-is-transforming-enterprise-customer-service/#1c9881991483 (accessed October 20, 2017).

CHAPTER 11

Conclusion

J. Mark Munoz and Al Naqvi

The advent and rise of artificial intelligence (AI) is an undeniable reality and an irreversible trend. It is true that in the short history of six or so decades of AI, several attempts were made to make the technology mainstream. Such attempts did not succeed. Dreams were shattered and investment wasted. But from the ashes of such failures emerged the modern AI revolution, which is not only sustainable but is also appearing as a formidable force in the world.

Artificial intelligence's strategic reach shapes productivity and a country's GDP (PWC 2016) and will positively impact several industries such as health care (data-based diagnostic support), automotive (autonomous fleets for ride sharing), financial services (personalized financial planning), retail and consumer (personalized design and production), technology, communication, and entertainment (media archiving and search), manufacturing (enhanced monitoring and auto-correction), energy (smart meters), transport and logistics (autonomous trucking) (PWC 2016).

In business, the advent of AI has redefined operations in areas relating to supply chain and logistics management, attention to customer needs, and the enhancement of digital experiences among many others (Popomaronis 2017).

The ability of AI to reconfigure business operations has led to dramatic results. For instance, NatureSweet, a U.S. company, formerly had employees walk around greenhouses to identify dying plants or insect infestations. This being a slow, laborious, and expensive process the firm decided to try integrating AI in their operations. Linking AI with cameras, they started monitoring the plants 24/7 and gathered instantaneous feedback (McFarland 2017).

On a daily basis, in companies all over the world, organizations are integrating AI in their businesses to boost operational efficiency. It has become an important tool and the means to understand their organization, market, industry, competition, and customers better.

Consequently as companies undertake efforts to improve and differentiate themselves, AI starts to play a critical role in the process. It elevates in importance from being a mere technological tool to a factor of strategic importance. Business strategy is about competitive advantage. In the past, competitive advantage was a function of industry structure, core competency, or facts such as differentiation. As society developed and the information revolution started, information and knowledge became the key factors in establishing a sustaining competitive advantage. The AI revolution, also known as the cognitive or the fourth industrial revolution, is redefining the rules of the game. Everything begins with the strategy of a firm. AI is no exception. However, AI should not be viewed as a tool, a factor, a driver, or a component of business strategy. It should be viewed as *the strategy*. In other words, companies should realize that their entire strategy at this time is and needs to be about the competitive dynamics unleashed by AI.

The featured chapters in this book highlight the fact that AI interfaces with key business operations. In particular, five realities are evident:

1. AI is an organization influencer—the use of AI in the organization impacts in operations in diverse ways. It alters the organization in one form or another.

2. AI is defined by the organization—the scale and scope of AI usage in an organization is defined by organizational attributes. For instance, an organization that has a strong ability for technological absorption or has a high cultural affinity for AI will likely progress faster in advancing AI in the firm.

3. Management drives AI—the extent of support from the management team will impact the pace in which AI will be used in the organization.

4. External factors affect an organization's AI performance—there are numerous factors that influence AI utilization in a company. These factors include the supporting infrastructure and architecture for the

relating to talent, culture, and technology are ready, and 4) thinking through appropriate governance and control measures (PWC 2016).

Table 11.2 highlights recommended courses of action organizations can take in an AI environment.

The strategic AI plan pointed out in Table 11.2 stresses the value of planning ahead for AI and creating a culture that encourages AI-related

Table 11.2 The strategic AI plan

Organizational need	Recommended action agenda
Organizations need to create a comprehensive AI plan.	Create a committee to develop a comprehensive strategic AI plan involving representatives from each department. This committee can evolve to become an AI circle and will continue explore ways to optimize the use of AI in the organization.
Reinvigorated marketing plan will be necessary.	Review existing marketing plans and identify areas of improvement.
Innovative organizational architecture involving new structures and policies will have to be created.	Review organizational structure and policies to create an AI-friendly or AI-compatible work environment. Provide AI-related training for all employees.
An AI unit within IT departments will need to be formed, alongside a top-level AI steering committee.	Develop AI specialists (AI-team) within the IT department who will be first responders on AI issues.
Finance and accounting departments will have to assimilate AI in their work systems.	Review existing financial plans and identify areas of improvement.
AI will need to be woven in the organization's ethical goals and strategies.	Create an AI ethical statement and a set of strategies.
Employees need to be motivated and rewarded for AI business ideas.	Offer rewards and merit pay increases for AI idea of the month as well as in participating in knowledge transfer.
Organizational structure and costs will need to be planned for as AI and robotics are used in organizations.	Embrace an AI culture by educating managers, employees, and organizational stakeholders on the merits of AI. Ensure participation in the AI circle.
Organizations can internationalize at a faster rate and scope, with ease of data gathering and analysis as a result of AI.	Review existing internationalization plans and identify areas of improvement.
Organizations need to integrate AI in their strategic plans, or create a comprehensive AI strategic plan.	Create a comprehensive strategic AI plan. Prepare to update and review results over time.

ideas in the organization. An environment that is AI-compatible will reap significant benefits relating to knowledge absorption, operational efficiencies, and cost savings among others.

In the process of strategic planning, organizations need to carefully anticipate potential barriers and strategize accordingly. Possible barriers include high cost and complexity of project implementation, legalities, employee training, and the management of information and data security. In fact, only about 20 percent of organizations possess the key skills to succeed with the AI technology (Rao 2017). Significant organizational assessment, risk planning, and thorough preparation have to be made.

The authors note that organizations have a choice in how they respond to the AI economy. Firms that plan ahead and strategically implement a well-conceived action plan will likely gain unique competitive advantages.

When the Internet arrived, many firms were unable to adjust. They found themselves lost and unable to comprehend the new dynamics. Blockbuster Video focused on expanding stores even when Netflix was designing alternative models. Bookstores all over the world did not see the emergence of Amazon as a threat until it was too late. Similarly, a tremendous change is taking place in the industry. The traditional auto sector seemed to be shocked by the rise of Tesla and autonomous cars. The pharmaceutical industry is rushing to embrace the technology to ward off competition from emerging AI firms. The traditional agri-businesses are acquiring AI companies to automate agriculture. The financial industry is embracing automated trading. All of these point to the beginning of what lies ahead.

It is important to note that the external environment in which the organization operates also impacts its ability to succeed in an AI environment. For example, government policies that support AI research and development or provide incentives for its usage can benefit companies. The presence or proximity of industries that sell AI-related goods and services can lower system acquisition costs. The quality of work and research in the industry shapes AI quality and performance. Available talent or expertise in AI through local universities affects the accessibility and quality of the organization's labor pool.

In support of business, governments need to take a proactive role to support the growth of AI. Mehr (2017) identified the need for governments to: (1) incorporate AI in their goals, (2) engage the citizenry, (3) build on existing resources, 4) consider data preparation, (5) manage ethical risks, and (6) strengthen employee potential.

Organizations would also benefit when the "AI ecosystem" is conducive to the expansion of AI. For instance, in communities where venture capitalists and bankers back AI, universities introduce AI courses and research labs, and the government offers tax breaks for AI initiatives—AI would likely flourish and dramatically contribute to company success.

The world of AI is a current reality and a cornerstone of the future. The market for AI is currently in its infancy with a size of only around $644 million in 2016, but this figure is expected to rise to $15 billion by 2022 (Rao 2017). AI will contribute approximately $15.7 trillion to the global economy by 2030 (PWC 2016).

Individuals, organizations, and countries have important roles to play and will shape the direction it takes. Planning for AI now, and pursuing a well-conceived strategic action, is definitely a step in the right direction.

References

McFarland, M. 2017. "Farmers Turn to Artificial Intelligence to Grow Better Crops." *CNN Tech*, available at http://money.cnn.com/2017/07/26/technology/future/farming-ai-tomatoes/index.html (accessed September 20, 2017).

Mehr, H. 2017. "Artificial Intelligence : 6 Steps Government Agencies Can Take." *State Scoop*, available at http://statescoop.com/artificial-intelligence-6-steps-government-agencies-can-take (accessed September 20, 2017).

Popomaronis, T. 2017. "11 Tech Leaders Share the Real Truth About Artificial Intelligence (and What Really Matters)." available at https://.forbes.com/sites/tompopomaronis/2017/08/29/11-tech-leaders-share-insights-on-artificial-intelligence-and-what-actually-matters/#2c7c758e6668 (accessed September 20, 2017).

PWC 2016. "Sizing the Prize. PWC's Global Artificial Intelligence Study: Exploiting the AI Revolution." available at https://.pwc.com/gx/en/issues/data-and-analytics/publications/artificial-intelligence-study.html (accessed September 21, 2017).

Rao, A. 2017. "A strategist's Guide to Artificial Intelligence." *Strategy + Business*, available at https://.strategy-business.com/article/A-Strategists-Guide-to-Artificial-Intelligence?gko=0abb5&utm_source=itw&utm_medium=20170523&utm_campaign=respB (accessed September 20, 2017).

About the Authors

Andrea Bencsik is a professor in a Hungarian university called Széchenyi István University in Győr and in J. Selye University in Slovakia. Her main research area is knowledge management and its connections with other processes and knowledge management system building in companies. She is a leader of an innovative research project, which aims to work out new ideas on how artificial intelligence can support knowledge management and be viably connected with various processes in a company.

Krishna Raj Bhandari is a final year doctoral student from the University of Vaasa, Finland. His dissertation revisits theories of Porter, Barney, and Coase in a panel data covering a period of 10 years. His recent research interest pertains to the assessment of the impact of information technology (IoT, cloud computing, and AI) on corporate strategy.

Sergio Biggemann is a senior lecturer in Business Marketing at the University of Otago.

Norrie J. Daroga is an engineer, lawyer, and seasoned executive, founder, and CEO of iDAvatars. He started his career at GE Healthcare and co-managed the listing of Metavante Technologies, Inc. (NYSE:MV) in 2007. iDAvatars builds interactive avatars, which have emotional intelligence and are used in self-directed applications as well health care management.

Margaret A. Goralski is a professor in the School of Business at Quinnipiac University. She has a Ph.D. in International Management from the International School of Management, Paris, France. Her current research interests include brain-based learning, business ethics, and ethics of artificial intelligence.

Mary Wanjiru Kinoti is a senior lecturer and associate dean, Graduate Business Studies, School of Business, University of Nairobi, Kenya. She holds a Ph.D.in Business Administration from the School of Business, University of Nairobi, in addition to Master of Business Administration (Marketing) and Bachelor of Commerce (Finance and Economics) degree. She has distinguished herself as a capable manager and administrator as coordinator of bachelor of commerce program, conferences, marketing, and branding activities within the school. She is a member of Marketing Society of Kenya, Kenya Institute of Management, as well as Academy of International Business (AIB) Sub-Saharan Africa chapter. Mary also consults for SMEs, public as well as private organizations in Kenya. She has co-authored book chapters on sustainable development, women empowerment, and entrepreneurship.

Krystyna Górniak-Kocikowska is a professor of Philosophy at Southern Connecticut State University. She has an MA in German Philology and a Ph.D. in Philosophy from Adam Mickiewicz University in Poznan, Poland. She also has an MA in Religious Studies from Temple University in Philadelphia, United States. Her current research interests include knowledge management, social, and ethical issues in the ICT-driven global society.

Carlos Vasquez is presently a Ph.D. candidate. He is an executive with 13 years of working experience in strategy, management, marketing, and particularly innovation areas. He is a recipient of a scholarship at the University of Sydney Business School, where he is conducting research on problem solving and innovation management.

Associate Professor **Abel Kinoti Meru** is the founding dean, Riara School of Business, Riara University, Kenya, and the founding chair of Academy of International Business Sub-Saharan Africa chapter. He holds a doctorate degree in Commerce from Nelson Mandela Metropolitan University, South Africa, an MBA (Marketing) and Bachelor of Commerce (Accounting) degrees. He is the author of a textbook on *"Business Incubation and Business Development in Kenya,"* co-edited a book on *The Changing Dynamics of International Business in Africa*, co-authored a book chapter in an upcoming edition on *Public Budgeting in African Nations*, and several articles published in local and international peer-reviewed journals.

J. Mark Munoz is a professor of International Business at Millikin University in Illinois, and a former visiting fellow at the Kennedy School of Government at Harvard University. He is a recipient of several awards including four Best Research Paper Awards, an international book award, a literary award, and the ACBSP Teaching Excellence Award among others. Aside from top-tier journal publications, he has authored/edited/co-edited 18 books such as: *Winning Across Borders, International Social Entrepreneurship, Contemporary Microenterprises: Concepts and Cases, Handbook on the Geopolitics of Business, Managerial Forensics, Advances in Geoeconomics* and *Global Business Intelligence*. He is chairman/CEO of the international management consulting firm Munoz and Associates International and chairman of the editorial board of the *Journal of Artificial Intelligence in Business, Policy, and Economy*. He serves as Advisor to the AI Initiative at the Kennedy School of Government at Harvard University.

Associate Professor **Felix Musau** is the founding dean, Riara School of Computing Sciences, Riara University, Kenya. He holds a Ph.D. and Master's in Computer Science and Technology from the Central South University, Peoples Republic of China. He has several publications in peer-reviewed journals in computing and information technology mainly on artificial intelligence, trust management, information security, and network management.

Al Naqvi is a big data strategist and a finance expert. Former CFO of a health care system, entrepreneur, and Fortune 500 executive, Naqvi has developed over 100 use cases in big data. Naqvi is also adjunct faculty member at Millikin where he teaches MBA Strategy course, a frequent speaker at conferences, and author of various articles and books. He is the founder and CEO of the American Institute of Artificial Intelligence.

Dr. Mehrdad Sharbaf is an adjunct professor at multiple universities, including Loyola Marymount, California State University, Dominguez Hills, and California State University, Northridge. His background includes more than 20 years of experience in industry and academia, focusing on disciplines such as system integration, system engineering, information security, and total quality information security management. During his career, he has taught at multiple institutions, including various educational institutions such as the previously mentioned colleges, as well as California State University, Long Beach, California State University, Los Angeles, and UCLA Extension. His research interests include quantum cryptography, quantum information processing, and total quality information security management, as well as network design and integration.

Luis A. Soto is a systems engineer, entrepreneur, and Latin-American guru in artificial intelligence and expert systems.

Index

OTHER TITLES IN THE STRATEGIC MANAGEMENT COLLECTION

John A. Pearce, Villanova University, Editor

- *First and Fast: Outpace Your Competitors, Lead Your Markets, and Accelerate Growth* by Stuart Cross
- *Strategies for University Management* by J. Mark Munoz and Neal King
- *Strategic Organizational Alignment: Authority, Power, Results* by Chris Crosby
- *Strategies for University Management, Volume II* by J. Mark Munoz and Neal King

Announcing the Business Expert Press Digital Library

Concise e-books business students need for classroom and research

This book can also be purchased in an e-book collection by your library as

- a one-time purchase,
- that is owned forever,
- allows for simultaneous readers,
- has no restrictions on printing, and
- can be downloaded as PDFs from within the library community.

Our digital library collections are a great solution to beat the rising cost of textbooks. E-books can be loaded into their course management systems or onto students' e-book readers.

The **Business Expert Press** digital libraries are very affordable, with no obligation to buy in future years. For more information, please visit **www.businessexpertpress.com/librarians**. To set up a trial in the United States, please email **sales@businessexpertpress.com**.

CPSIA information can be obtained
at www.ICGtesting.com
Printed in the USA
BVHW08s1052170918
527713BV00020B/339/P